THE PULSE GLASS

BY THE SAME AUTHOR

Veronica —

The Pulse Glass

And the beat of other hearts

Gillian Tindall

Gillian Tindall

2/12/19

Chatto & Windus

LONDON

1 3 5 7 9 10 8 6 4 2

Chatto & Windus, an imprint of Vintage,
20 Vauxhall Bridge Road,
London SW1V 2SA

Chatto & Windus is part of the Penguin Random House group
of companies whose addresses can be found at
global.penguinrandomhouse.com.

Penguin
Random House
UK

First published by Chatto & Windus in 2019

penguin.co.uk/vintage

A CIP catalogue record for this book is available from the British Library

ISBN 9781784742997

Typeset in 12/16.5 pt Adobe Jenson Pro
by Integra Software Services Pvt. Ltd, Pondicherry

Printed and bound in Great Britain by Clays Ltd, Elcograf S.p.A.

Penguin Random House is committed to a sustainable future
for our business, our readers and our planet. This book is
made from Forest Stewardship Council® certified paper.

MIX
Paper from
responsible sources
FSC® C018179

This book is dedicated to my husband
and lifetime companion, Richard Lansdown

Question put to Prof. Paul M. Cobb of Pennsylvania University:

'What is your favourite archive?'
Answer: 'That box you discover in your grandparents' attic.'
History Today, June 2017

Those who knew
what was going on here
must make way for
those who know little.
And less than little.
And finally as little as nothing.
'The End and the Beginning' by Wislawa Szymborska
(translated by Joanna Trzeciak)

So the little woolwork picture had gone at last – in its own good time ... During its existence it had given pleasure to a number of people, which is mainly what things are for ...

Now the possibility of its ever having an effect of any kind upon any human being again seemed gone ...

A Dog So Small by Philippa Pearce

But when from a long-distant past nothing subsists after the people are dead, after the things are broken and scattered ... the smell and taste of things remain poised a long time, like souls ... amid the ruins of all the rest; and bear unfaltering, in the tiny and almost impalpable drop of their essence, the vast structure of recollection.

À la Recherche du Temps Perdu by Marcel Proust

CONTENTS

CHAPTER I

The Down-Train to Childhood

On a Good Friday in April, in the second decade of the twenty-first century, I go to sprinkle ashes along the stones, primroses, bluebells and last year's leaves of an abandoned railway line in Sussex that has become a path for walkers and cyclists.

Human ashes are flecked pale grey and white, like a large stock of pearl necklaces chopped up and mixed with clean dust. They pour dry and smooth, leaving only the faintest floury residue on the hands. While they are packed tightly into the bag supplied by the crematorium, this concentrated, irreducible residue of an adult human being, these chips of bone, weigh only about six or seven pounds, the weight of a newborn baby.

When this man, who is now ash, was born, some ten days earlier than the expected date, he weighed just over seven pounds. A very cold morning at the start of a winter just after the end of the Second World War, which was to turn into one of the worst winters of the century. A few years later, when we sang at school near Christmas time ' ... *earth stood hard as iron, water like a stone*', it made me think of that winter, which has

now receded so far, out of most living memories, that the carol
fits it still more closely:

> *Snow had fallen, snow on snow, sn-oow on sn-oow …*
> *In the bleak mid-winter, lo-oong ag-oo*

Long ago. In the cold house in Sussex near Ashdown Forest –
all houses were cold, long ago, unless you were right by the
kitchen or sitting-room fire – I am fast asleep in my own room.
Then, suddenly, I am awake, and someone is standing by my
bed:

'You've got a little brother!'

Great excitement. I am hustled into my dressing gown. As
we cross the landing to my mother's bedroom I encounter a
familiar doctor-figure, in black jacket and pin-striped trousers,
just leaving. 'Hello, Mary-Jane!' he says. He calls all boys John-
Thomas and all girls Mary-Jane. It makes life simpler for him,
he says.

My mother is in bed, tucked up, looking quite ordinary, which
surprises me rather. Beside her is the long-promised baby,
cocooned in a small, woven orange blanket, which I know has
been sent by an aunt all the way from Orkney. Such presents
were valuable and prized, in 1946.

That blanket survived time and chance, and the disintegration
of our home when I was seventeen and the baby boy not yet
nine. When I was a young woman I adopted it as a shawl, and
later as a wrap for my own son. A generation further on, it was
still with me and served to cocoon my first grandson, but
somehow between his infancy and the birth of another one four
years later it disappeared, perhaps to some other, unknown baby.

*

Most objects, like all people, disappear in the end. Even in a country as relatively peaceful as the British Isles, which has endured neither invasion nor civil war for several hundred years, there are few possessions more than one hundred and fifty years old, and most are far, far more recent.

Yet already, by the eighteenth century, three hundred years ago, we had in Britain a burgeoning middle class larger than that of any other European country, and replete with possessions. These people, both the well-to-do and the aspirant 'middling sort', were, by the days of the Hanoverians, doing quite nicely, thank you. Wills, and still more probate inventories, reveal a mass of sheer stuff, all valued and obsessively itemised. The consumerism that would develop in the wake of the industrial revolution and the unprecedented wealth of the Victorian Empire still lay in the future, but, looking from our side of time, signs of its approach were already apparent. Adam Smith, the author of *The Wealth of Nations* (1776), remarked that even quite modest British homes frequently contained objects brought or copied from the other side of the world, thanks to the energies of the East India, Levant and Hudson Bay Companies. This was at a time when the mainly-rural people of other European countries were still fabricating everything for their own use, with the sole exceptions of iron and salt. British families had Delft plates and English imitations of the same, dresses made of Indian cotton and Kashmir shawls. They had copper pots and pewter ones. People slightly higher up the social scale had silver forks and spoons. They had cloudy mirrors and decorated tea-caddies and miniature writing desks, and books – for they could mostly read. The most prosperous had

engravings and even portraits in oils, and cloaks lined with fur
from the Baltic, lockets and brooches and a great deal of closely
guarded silk and lace, and necessary thick-felted wool to protect
against time and chance …

Gone. Nearly all of it. The materials consumed stickily with
moth-eggs and damp, or passed on to poorer people and thence
to still poorer ones, finally becoming rags for cleaning. The furniture, once outmoded, discarded, uncherished, abandoned to
servants' rooms or to the poor, scratched and broken and in the
end chopped up for firewood. Here and there a locket survives,
a little battered, containing a curl of who-knows-whose hair; or
a Bible, worn with use, inscribed with forgotten names; or some
silver spoons, thinned with use – generations of soups and jellies
and creams. Or, occasionally, a portrait, once an affectionate or
proud link with a grandmother or wealthy cousin, now reduced
down and down over the generations to a Lady Unknown.

Some things, though, do not disappear but, rather, change their
essence: their very meaning is transformed. I go back, for a little
while, to the railway line in Sussex.

Its modest embankments and cuttings are likely to last
through the centuries even as the traces of Roman roads have
done, but its sleepers and rails have vanished now as completely
as has the little boy whose birth I recall and whose happiest
childhood memory was of playing alongside them. These memories were to condition his whole later life, for he became, both
in work and in leisure, a railway man. But by the time he was
grown-up, the down-train to childhood was no longer running.

From far off we would hear the whistle of one of the steam-
engines that, about ten times a day, would make its way with

frequent stops from Three Bridges, or from distant, improbable Victoria, passing not far from our home to its eventual destination at Tunbridge Wells. The little boy, N, would clutch a hand – mine, or that of an attendant adult – in delighted anticipation as we removed ourselves a few feet from the track when the rails began to hum. The engine, when it finally appeared, would at first seem friendly but then grow in size, becoming enormous, a dragon twenty foot high that crashed past with such a din and a fleeting blast of heat that we would cower back in spite of ourselves.

There was a lane there with a level-crossing, on which we laid the ha'pennies that had been currency for a hundred years or more to see if the train's passage would squash them out into mock-pennies. On cue, before the train appeared out of the tree-lined cutting, but when a message had pinged down the wires and its puffing could just be heard, a short, stout lady would appear out of the crossing-keeper's cottage. If the white wooden gates were open to the lane, she would swing them shut against the occasional cart or van, to let the train pass.

And sometimes, if the train was an 'up' one, going the other way to mythic London, and we had timed our excursion right, there would be a farm vehicle already waiting in the lane and a full milk-churn or two standing on a kind of giants' coffee-table near the track. The train, snorting frustrated smoke, would slow and slow till, as it was creeping past the crossing, the guard on board who was standing at an open door, together with a farm labourer on the ground, would rapidly hoist the churns into the guard's van. The labourer jumped back, the guard waved to the watching engine-driver or fireman, the driver tooted and the train picked up speed again. This century-old evening exercise of ingenuity, manual strength and timing must then have been in its final years.

Today, this memory seems as antique as the exploits in E. Nesbit's *The Railway Children* of a hundred years ago, or of Hardy's *Tess of the d'Urbervilles* set fifty years before that. Country railways, even the still-living ones, carry a message of nostalgia today, and the dead ones far more so. Remote, derelict stations where empty grates yawn in the darkened waiting rooms, and sheep crop the grassed-over platforms, speak of a lost land of innocence. But then so do the lived-in ones, where geranium pots decorate the sootless walls and the one-time track is burgeoning with potato plants and runner beans. Forgotten is the fact that, close to, the trains could be terrifying and, indeed, lethal: in memory they are reduced to lovable, gentle elephants, to Thomas the Tank Engine, Edward, Gordon and the rest, from the stories of the Reverend W. Awdry.

Very different was the view of the Iron Road when railways began to spread across the British Isles in the 1840s. This new and extraordinary development, which happened a little earlier in Britain than it did across the wider and more mountainous expanses of the Continent, was perceived, correctly, as a threat to a way of life that had lasted for centuries. Over time, change had always occurred, but it had been gradual and incremental. Narrow packhorse tracks had, through the centuries, broadened into gravel highways, towns had begun to extend beyond their defensive walls. By the eighteenth century ancient market towns, to which the country around had made its way on foot or by cart, were becoming bustling destinations for long-range coaches. New turnpike roads were built, and long-established ale-houses found themselves happily at the centre of a whole network of coach-stops and horse-team changes and the feeding and bedding of travellers.

But the railways had different priorities and requirements. They cut across old routes, linking one new manufacturing centre with another, ignoring venerable hilltop towns, bypassing historical centres whose traditional wool or linen trades were seen to be in decline. Inns that had, for two or three generations, seen scores of coaches from competing companies in and out of their stable-yards every twenty-four hours, found an odd quietness descending. Some traditional coaching routes, such as the one today followed north-west by the A65 between Yorkshire and Lancashire, by which Charlotte Brontë's young Jane Eyre is sent alone on the long journey to school at 'Lowood' (Cowan Bridge), became so quiet that grass grew over their stones.

Many people welcomed the railway excitedly, delighted at the opportunities it brought for expanded trade and more, and much cheaper, travel. Coaches had never been cheap, and each one, even with its roof crammed with male travellers, could carry at the most a dozen passengers at a time. A railway train could carry hundreds, and soon did. But those who feared the railways, with their danger, their noise, their dirt and their speed and the way they cut one old field or woodland off from another – who feared that the railways would destroy old patterns of living, thinking and moving about, and in doing so destroy communities – were of course right. Trains bore no relationship to the countryside through which they passed. The alienation of the train traveller from the land or towns through which he was carried was remarked on by a shocked Ruskin, and perceived all too accurately by Dickens in a famous passage in *Dombey and Son*:

Through the hollow, on the height, by the heath, by the orchard, by the park, by the garden, over the canal, across the river, where the sheep are feeding, where the mill is going, where the barge is floating, where the dead are lying, where the factory is smoking, where the stream is running, where the village clusters, where the great cathedral rises, where the bleak moor lies, and the wild breeze soothes or ruffles it at its inconstant will; away with a shriek, and a roar, and a rattle, and no trace to leave behind but dust and vapour …

Away and still away, onward and onward ever; glimpses of cottage-homes, of houses, mansions, rich estates, of husbandry and handicraft, of people, of old roads and paths that look deserted, small and insignificant as they are left behind; and so they do, and what else is there but such glimpses in the track of the indomitable monster, Death!

The possibility of death that is unmistakably present in the overpowering physical presence of the locomotive becomes also, in the course of this passage (in its entirety far longer than is quoted here), the death implicit in time itself, charging ahead, constantly obliterating and eradicating what has been, carrying us into the unknown.

It was no personal oddity that led Dickens to set much of his fiction slightly back in time to the pre-railway era: Thackeray did the same, and so did the Brontë sisters. Evidently, by the middle decades of the nineteenth century, that bygone-but-so-recent time was felt to be a dateless setting more suitable for fiction than the immediate, nerve-rackingly evolving present.

And in addition to the alienation from real place and the social dislocation that was perceived to come as the result of the trains, there was, more prosaically, the blight cast by the sheer construction of stations, coaling bays and shunting yards. In an article published in his magazine *All the Year Round* in 1860, Dickens wrote:

> I left Dullborough in the days when there were no railroads in the land, I left it in a stage coach ... [when I arrived back by train] I began to look about me; and the first discovery I made was, that the Station had swallowed up the playing field.
>
> It was gone. The two beautiful hawthorn trees, the hedge, the turf, and all those buttercups and daisies, had given place to the stoniest of jolting roads: while, beyond the Station, an ugly dark monster of a tunnel kept its jaws open, as if it had swallowed them and were ravenous for more destruction. The coach that had carried me away was melodiously called Timpson's Blue-Eyed Maid, and belonged to Timpson, at the coach-office, up-street; the locomotive engine that had brought me back was called severely No. 97, and belonged to SER, and was spitting ashes and hot water over the blighted ground.

It was the initial shocking mainline network that spread in the 1840s which changed provincial life for ever. The next big wave of railway enthusiasm, some twenty years later, brought fewer fundamental changes and was more generally welcomed. The public knew about trains by then – knew they didn't give you brain-fever, lead to revolution or upset the weather – and had come to think that it might be rather a good idea if their particular village could have its own line linking up with an existing junction. So hamlets that had, till then, huddled inwards around churches and village greens, found themselves endowed with small stations, usually at a little distance across the fields. Footbridges were built over cuttings and low tunnels under embankments, to allow cows to pass from one meadow to the other. Each station was given decorative barge-boarding, a parcels office, coal depot, signal box, stationmaster's house, running water and often gas lighting too – the new amenities of modern life, which would be potentially available to the village also. 'Station Roads' grew between the old cottages and the new installation, and Desirable Residences sprinkled themselves along this carriageway. The social composition of rural Britain changed. Now that the monied classes could 'run up to town' so easily, they were more inclined to settle for country living. Ordered goods could be delivered from afar in a way impossible in horse-and-cart days. Gentlemen inclined for a day's hunting could come down on the early milk-train. A bright country boy could travel daily to the grammar school in the nearest town. Coachmen who had lost their jobs when the old stage-routes disintegrated took to driving short-distance flys instead, the station taxis of the time. Rural England was transformed, but most people were by now quite pleased with the transformation.

Fifty years or so later, in the first decades of the twentieth century, the gently weathered rural station, often beautified with sunflowers or geraniums grown by the not-overburdened stationmaster, had become a conventional part of life. The world without railways had passed from human memory. In Sussex, husbands in business suits travelled up and down to London daily, convinced that they 'lived in the country', that mark of social status, savouring the early tweet of birds as they hurried stationwards in the half-light of dawn, and the short pleasure in the summer months of arriving back twelve hours later with the sun not yet set. Already, decades before the country railways would be closed down in the face of ever-increasing car use, they had developed an aura of gentle tradition, a whiff of nostalgia for a vanished past even before they were officially regarded as obsolete. When their doom was pronounced, around 1960, the shock to the communities they had served was considerable, and the indignation engendered is not extinct today.

For a while, the dead railway lines became a forerunner of the industrial dereliction and neglect that would blight Britain over the next generation. I recall walking over the Sussex line of my childhood some dozen years after it had been closed. Along the embanked sections one could stride as on a dyke, but in the cuttings the mud left behind by the removal of the track was soft, lush with toadstools and dock leaves, and under the bridges stood great pools of water. Impossible to believe that, not very many years before, trains had run through these lost valleys many times a day. And impossible, too, *not* to believe that the living railway, which I remembered clearly and had taken for granted, was still there, on some alternative circuit of reality. In one derelict station tall yarrows were growing up through rifts in the cement platform. More disconcertingly still, a few miles further on, the station most familiar to me had vanished utterly, as if a giant had scissored it out of an otherwise complete scene. It took me a moment to realise that in fact the station buildings had been demolished into rubble and used as hardcore to fill in the space between the platforms: a site, no doubt, for some other future building, some other life.

Not far away from where the station had been, I noticed, and remembered, a handsome thatched-roof farmhouse complete with barns. There, I recalled, I had been taken to buy eggs in the earliest time, before my brother was born or imagined. There were Italian prisoners-of-war employed there then, small, dark, friendly men of whom I was shy. They showed us some pigs, and a family of fluffy goslings, which I did not believe were going to turn into bold, frightening geese.

By the 1970s, when I took my long walk, with the station and the noise of trains gone, the one-time farmyard had become a smooth lawn with white-painted chairs on it. The eldest son of the old farming couple had become a prosperous local builder. But today, decades later again, I hear that the place is a farm once more, a 'biodynamic community venture', employing traditional methods of animal husbandry that the old couple with their prisoners-of-war labourers would recognise. There long before the railway came to bisect its home fields, this once-humble but substantial country dwelling had turned out to be far more lasting.

The dereliction, too, has all passed now. The one-time railroad has been smoothed and gravelled and re-baptised the 'Forest Way'. Trees arch over it; bluebells and primroses, and the ox-eye daisies and buttercups that Dickens thought had been driven away by iron and stones, by ashes and hot water, have returned. To receive, one Good Friday, ashes of another kind.

The level-crossing gates have gone and so has the keeper's cottage. Up and down the Way, in Easter-holiday peace, come intermittent families with children on bicycles, devotees of safety and green living. They can know nothing of milk-churns or of the little boy in grey flannel shorts who used to stand here in delighted anticipation of the coming train. The railway that was once taken for an archetype of destruction, *the indomitable monster, Death*', has by the sheer passing of time become a

peaceful site of natural renewal, for which forgetting is a necessary element.

But not all axed lines are consigned to oblivion, for the railroad
of the past can also create its own timeless afterlife. The British,
the original builders of railways, are notable for their attachment
to them. There are today more preserved and revived stretches of
steam-line in the British Isles than anywhere else in the world.
On these lines the Railway Age continues in a blessed afterlife,
where the brass is always shining, trains are always on time (or
if they aren't, it doesn't matter), employees are always smiling
and there is Mazawattee still for tea in chipped but imperish-
able enamel. The Forest Way ends in East Grinstead, and there,
from the station – a real station, this one, connected to London
Victoria – you can today access the line to Horsted Keynes.
Once, it was just another obscure Sussex country branch line,
then a derelict one. Now it is the world-famous Bluebell Line.
Its tree-hung embankments are a haven for birds and other small
wildlife such as dormice, since the intermittent noise of the trains
scares off larger predators.

On this odd bank holiday, this Easter time of waiting, as we
arrive back at the real station there is a crowd a hundred yards
away at the entrance to the Bluebell Line, and a cloud of authentic
steam. It turns out to be the Flying Scot of the 1920s paying a
regal visit.

My brother was, as he said himself, 'an anorak', an authority
on steam-trains around the world. While briskly organising
modern-day freight traffic, he permanently regretted steam's
passing. What a pity, I thought, he's not with us, though he's
probably seen the Flying Scot many times ... But, since he was

now mysteriously, unexpectedly and for ever absent, I felt happy to have seen a grand old locomotive of the sort he loved that same afternoon.

Among the things he left behind, unfinished, was an elaborate, beautifully constructed scale layout, complete with miniature houses and stations that he had made himself, stone-chip by stone-chip. It was the model of a railway line in Lowland Scotland that was planned in detail in the 1860s but never actually built, and of which he had acquired the detailed designs.

Only when he was suddenly dead, and the layout would therefore be abandoned even as the plan for the life-size one was, did a memory of another dream-railway of his come back to me, from very early in his childhood. He was perhaps not yet three, still sleeping in a cot, and when our mother came to lift him out of it one morning he said with delighted anticipation, 'Let's go and see the train in the drawing room!'

She cast doubt on there being any train in the drawing room, but he was insistent, so she carried him downstairs. There was of course no train, and tears of bitter disappointment followed. I wonder now if the superlative miniature dream-train-that-never-was, a celestial version of the ancient Hornby train that was his favourite toy, lodged in a corner of his mind that long-ago morning in infancy and was never displaced.

CHAPTER II

Vanished Doorways

Notoriously, people avoid thinking about the inescapable fact of their own death. They act, and even speak, as if mortality were, with luck and good management, avoidable, or at least endlessly postponable. This unwillingness to confront a basic fact of human existence is probably far more widespread today than it was in past eras, when mortal sickness struck readily and an accident that now would be a passing misfortune could bring a life to an end. Rather, the mental agility of our ancestors seems to have been devoted not to pretending that death was escapable, but to trying to avoid the worst aspects of what lay beyond death, as recounted by the Church.

I will not venture into the shifting intricacies of Judgement as presented over the centuries. The idea that souls would all be arbitrarily sorted into the saved and the damned clearly presented a moral problem on all but the crudest of assessments. Hence, no doubt, the invention of a third place, Purgatory – in literal terms, a purifying system to prepare sinners for Heaven. The concept seems to have been mooted in the seventh century, and to have been borrowed from older faith systems, but it only acquired official status in the late twelfth. A hundred years later again Saint Thomas Aquinas promoted the idea of Purgatory as being located in an actual, physical space on Earth, and Dante followed this vision. But the sense that the Last Judgement, rather than being an ongoing business, was a yet-to-come, once-and-for-all grand occasion that would not take place till the Last Trump sounded created further problems regarding the status of the warehoused souls. How fair was it that the long dead should still be languishing interminably in Purgatory, awaiting their call, if the End of Days was near and the recently dead would only have a short spell there?

More sophisticated thought in some quarters favoured the idea that the length or shortness of earthly time was irrelevant to the way time might be perceived by a soul on the far side of death, regardless of which of the three realms it found itself in. But this again hardly fitted in with the system, much promoted during the Middle Ages by certain religious communities, whereby Purgatorial time could be shortened if Masses for the dead soul were said or instigated by the living. This inevitably led to a brisk commerce in the sale of what were called 'Indulgences', in effect a trade in paid-for prayers, to enable the well-to-do to shorten the Purgatorial sentence for themselves or for other family members. For by that time Purgatory itself seems to have acquired so many of the characteristics of Hell – fire, brimstone, unspeakable torments – as to be indistinguishable from it. Fire had, in any case, always been recognised as an agent of purification, as the medieval Lyke-Wake Dirge testifies:

> From Brig o'Dread when thou may'st pass
>   Every nighte and alle.
> To Purgatory fire thou com'st at last
>   And Christe receive thy saule.

Was there, therefore, a distinction to be made between fire and fire? If the dead person had done good works in life, or his family were subscribing to the Church on his behalf –

> The fire sall never make thee shrink;
>   And Christe receive thy saule

– Otherwise it might 'burn thee to the bare bane ...'

The Reformation in England put paid to all this. The sale of Indulgences by the Catholic Church was a particular target for Protestant condemnation. Indeed you might think, from the story of the Reformation as recounted over many generations in British schoolrooms with a Church of England orientation, that the sale of Indulgences by 'fat, greedy monks' was a major cause of the tornado of passionate belief, counter-belief, accusation and counter-accusation that swept the whole of Europe for the best part of two hundred years. But in any case the idea of souls awaiting the Last Judgement never seems to have caught on in the popular imagination, however much certain Christian sects promoted it. The prospect of being kept in suspension after death, even benignly, for hundreds – possibly thousands –

of earthly years, waiting to discover your fate, evidently struck people as illogical, and this becomes clear in traditional speech patterns.

In the imaginations of believers down the centuries, and still today, the known and loved dead are not in Purgatory or any other form of celestial waiting room. They are already 'Up there', 'With God, which is far better', 'Asleep in Jesus', 'Free from this Vale of Tears', 'Gone to a Better Place' and numerous other circumlocutions. On tombstones from the late eighteenth and nineteenth centuries, a time when worldly calculations seem to have implied a special, Protestant form of Indulgence, inscriptions quite frequently suggest that precisely because the dead party (as well as being an ornament to society) never failed to trust in the Life Everlasting, that Life he or she must certainly have found. No wonder loss of faith assumed a particular horror when it brought with it the corollary that precisely because you had lost it, you would be outcast from the heavenly equivalent of good society. Socio-religious selection may be far less rigorous today, but a walk round any cemetery will still show that the dead are not elsewhere in some unguessable Other World, but have just 'Gone on Ahead for a little while': 'Till we meet again', '*Encore un peu de temps je vous reverrai*', 'Till the shadows fall and we are reunited', 'I have just gone into a nearby room', 'His wife, who joined him on ... [such-and-such a date]', 'Together once more.'

Indeed, it struck me when I was a child, and rather given to reflective wanders round the local cemetery, that much of the standard religion to which most adults then appeared to subscribe seemed to be devoted to promoting a view of the Afterlife as a recognisable, if improved version of life on Earth.

When, one day, I asked my grandmother if she thought Heaven was really there (my parents seemed evasive and unenthusiastic on the subject: I was canvassing further opinion), she said: 'Oh, I do hope so, darling. I should so like to see dear Ethel [her elder sister] again. And George and Guy, too, of course ...' Her voice trailed off, and I could make a childish guess at where her thoughts had gone. Her redoubtable husband, my grandfather, was still very much alive, but being many years older than her was clearly likely to die first. In all honesty, my grandmother could hardly say, 'And perhaps Hughie will be there waiting for me, too.' Hughie's lifelong atheism, that of a clever young man-about-town of the 1890s, was well known to all, even to me.

My brother N received, as I did, the then-standard school Christian education: morning assembly with hymns and prayers, Scripture lessons, Confirmation classes. Since, by then, our mother had died by her own hand, such bland fare was hardly likely to impress him. And I do not think that he dared ask anyone, or that anyone dared embark for him, on what happens to suicides after death. They should have. But probably they funked it.

Only as a middle-aged man, many years later, did he become interested in matters one might characterise as philosophical or spiritual. Christianity did not appeal to him, but he evolved a belief system of his own. He did not like to talk about it much, but it seemed to involve reincarnation, of a rather special kind. Worldwide, the religious beliefs that incorporate reincarnation (Hinduism and Buddhism) are subscribed to by many millions. Certainly the logic of reincarnation seems appealing, and less opaque than the Christian Heaven-or-Hell dichotomy. However, in my brother's version of it, reincarnation did not apparently work in the standard way, with a life of honest endeavour leading to an upgrade in the next one, or a life devoted to selfishness and unconcern for others resulting to demotion to a beast of burden next time round. It could not work in this morally consequential way because chronology itself, it seemed, was obliterated in my brother's reincarnatory scheme, in which you might as easily be moved back in time as forward.

'Do you really mean,' I asked, having digested this, 'that in your next life you could be a medieval knight, or monk, or ... Or a Victorian engine-driver?'

He smiled. and said, 'That's what I'm hoping for!'

I do not know how much he really meant this and how much it was a daydream, but it was clear that, behind the joke, some fundamental and complex belief was there. Possibly it related to the very ancient concept of serial time (revived in the twentieth century by J.W. Dunne)[1] in which key events are repeated and repeated, to good or ill effect, till some cycle is exhausted and a further one can begin.

But, if I am not careful, I shall find I have pre-empted my whole theme of memory, loss and the arbitrary survival of a few objects. If we consign the whole concept of the past to a many-dimensional timelessness, we lose it in any sense in which it still holds meaning for us. And, in practice, none of us behave as if all time were eternally present. A sense of time moving in one direction is the wavelength on which we live. My brother lived day-to-day on that wavelength as much as anyone else, and more than many: tokens of the past were precious to him. From his days as a young railway employee in distant Scotland and then as a world traveller, he had collected enamel advertisements, station signs, name plates, engine plates to which, over the years, rarity and value accrued. Many were carefully itemised and bestowed in his Will, which was made in haste on his marriage in middle life and then never revisited, so that some of the intended recipients were dead themselves when the moment came or simply lost to sight, another effect of time ... In other respects his Will was sketchy to the point of inadequacy. He had not expected to die with utter suddenness, lying down at the end of the morning in the clothes he had worn for a brisk walk, a few weeks before his seventieth birthday.

He had not expected, either, to leave, to a further destiny of incompleteness, the scale layout of the never-actually-built railway line between Dumfries and Stranraer. In a specially constructed cabin down his garden he had been busy, with huge care and talent, re-creating a past that had never actually existed but, with a very slight alteration to reality, would have done so. In this, he was in the role of the beggar in J-L. Borges's story.[2] There was an ancient doorway, which survived as long as it was regularly visited by a beggar, but after his death the doorway disappeared ...

It is the vanished doorways to the past that concern me, and the traces of them that survive that are the materials of this account. A handful of objects, obsolete, broken or discarded. Autolycus's 'alms for oblivion' that get stashed haphazardly in Time's wallet;[3] but which are sometimes transformed when time itself bestows on them more durable meanings.

An intricate model engine, standing quiet on its unfinished rails; once-cherished letters whose writers and recipients alike have slipped over the edge of living memory; a broken ivory saint; unnamed photographs; a painted plate; a well-used street-map; a wooden house-beam that once sailed the ocean; fragments of carved stone or painted glass; a bird's nest thirty years old; a few minutes of very early film; a miniature sand-glass that once counted the beat of innumerable extinguished hearts; a small leather handbag ... These are the talismans through which I attempt, fleetingly, to retrieve the huge complexity of the past. An enormous wealth of vanished lives.

CHAPTER III

Everything Exists

I am sitting in a private office in the British Library, the admirably unpretentious red-brick building that stands in the Euston Road on the site of a one-time goods yard for St Pancras Station. The rails were themselves laid on the site of a sprawling slum generally known as Agar Town that, for a brief nineteenth-century generation, colonised these meadows of St Pancras manor, before being swept away again.

A few years ago, when excavations were going on behind the library in preparation for building the Crick medical research centre, archaeologists found little, so thoroughly had the laying out of the goods yard wiped signs of earlier occupation. But from a truncated drainpipe, which must have belonged to a sink in one of the wash-houses of Agar Town and been missed by the railway engineers, they retrieved: a tin teaspoon, a small medicine bottle of thick green glass, part of a tiny broken wooden horse and a cheap locket on a broken chain. Did some young child, long ago, have a fatal passion for pushing small objects down the mysterious plug-hole? The owner of the locket, in particular, must have hunted for it.

I am sitting in a private office in the library because a contemporary, known to me for decades and now a distinguished figure in the library hierarchy, has something to show me. He places in my hands a small, compact book bound in red goatskin, hardly bigger than an old-style British passport and considerably fatter. If it were a hundred and fifty years old, one would say it was in good condition, considering its age, only the spine a little battered. In fact it is over thirteen hundred years old, the oldest book in the Western world to survive in its original binding. And its excellent condition is all the more remarkable in that it is known to have spent four hundred years in the coffin of Saint Cuthbert of Lindisfarne. It is, not surprisingly, almost the most expensive book ever to have been sold, and my friend is delighted because the National Heritage Memorial Fund, along with several other charitable trusts, has come forward with most of the £9 million needed for the library to buy the book from the monks of Stonyhurst College in Lancashire.

'I thought you'd like to see it,' he said.

I can hardly believe my good fortune in holding briefly in my hands such a unique, extraordinary object – and yet one so simple and so untouched by time that its very presence seems to wipe out centuries. Its cover has an embossed formal design reminiscent of a flower. It has in the text none of the elaborate illuminated letters we associate with the Lindisfarne Gospels, which are thought to have been made slightly later, possibly to celebrate Cuthbert's canonisation. It is a copy of St John's Gospel in Latin, written out by a monk in late-seventh-century pure uncial script.

In those early Christian days, islands that we now regard as remote outposts of the United Kingdom were, in comparison with almost everywhere else, easy to reach. Being readily accessible by sea, they were more conveniently situated as religious centres than were mainland places surrounded by forests, swamps and trackless hills and dales. The Lindisfarne Island brotherhood was established with the conversion to Christianity of Northumbria by the Irish saint Aidan. Cuthbert became his successor, an early bishop and companion to kings. He died on one of the Farne Islands in 698, and was buried in Lindisfarne. Pilgrimages were made to his grave, miraculous cures were reported (such were PR practices in early Christian days) and at the end of eleven years, when it had been planned to place his skeletal remains in a shrine, his coffin was opened. But to everyone's surprise and delight, the body was intact, unrotted. Evidently the dry, sandy soil of the island had mummified it, and therefore clothes and other small objects that had accompanied him to the tomb were unspoiled by body liquor – further indications of Cuthbert's sainthood. It was probably at this point that the small Gospel, which seems to have been created in the fellow-Northumbrian monastery at Jarrow, home to the Venerable Bede, was bestowed as a gift and placed upon Cuthbert's breast.

For the next ninety years pilgrimages were made to the tomb, but in the summer of 793 Viking raiders came, plundered gold and silver, killed some of the monks and took younger ones and boys as slaves. Saint Cuthbert was luckily undisturbed, and the monastery struggled on for another eighty years or so, but there were further raids and in 875 it was decided to abandon the place. The coffin with Saint Cuthbert in it, along with a few other remaining treasures, was carried across the tidal causeway that links Lindisfarne with the mainland for only part of each day. Then began a hundred-year odyssey, as the coffin was carried from place to place, with what must have been tremendous effort and subterfuge, to keep it safe from the Vikings. Finally it found refuge in Durham. There, after the Norman Conquest, Benedictine monks replaced 'the Saint Cuthbert's folk' and in the following generation the great Norman cathedral was built. A grand new shrine was made for Saint Cuthbert and, before placing him in it, the monks opened the coffin again to make sure the body and its accessories were still intact – which they were. At this point the book seems to have been taken out and, still regarded as precious, lent occasionally to a distinguished visitor to wear in a bag round the neck.

Once more, pilgrims visited. Another four centuries passed. But then came the Reformation, with the Dissolution of the Monasteries and the destruction of innumerable documents, carvings and shrines. The coffin was again opened; the body was still apparently entirely recognisable, but it was left lying in the vestry and does not seem to have survived this final exposure to the air, since what was later reburied inconspicuously behind the high altar was a skeleton. It was at some point in the downgrading of sainthood that the Gospel bound in red goatskin vanished – possibly tucked surreptitiously inside the jerkin of an Old Believer who wanted to make sure that the book at least survived.

Thereafter the sturdy little book followed a slightly mysterious and scantily documented path. Durham Cathedral Priory's library remained in existence, unlike most monastery libraries in those troubled times, but the Gospel does not seem to have been added to it. It crops up next in the early seventeenth century in the possession of a book collector in Oxford, a Fellow of Trinity College which, before the Reformation, had belonged to the monks of Durham. Its whereabouts in the next phase of ideological destructiveness, under Oliver Cromwell, is not clear: I suspect it was moved about discreetly from one recusant family to another, for it reappears again in the eighteenth century in the possession of the third Earl of Lichfield. Although he was a Privy Councillor and eventually Chancellor of the University of Oxford, this archetypal English nobleman was known in his own circle to be a Catholic sympathiser. He apparently gave the book to Thomas Phillips, a Catholic convert and sometime Jesuit, who later in life modified his allegiance and became chaplain in an English great house. Later again, Phillips made his peace with the Jesuits, returned to their fold and bequeathed the book to the English Jesuit Society, which was then based in Liège. After the Revolution in 1789, these Jesuits fled from France – and founded Stonyhurst College.

There the Gospel seems to have remained as a prized possession till, in the late twentieth century, those in charge of Stonyhurst evidently decided that this inconspicuous object was too impossibly valuable to remain permanently in their care. They lent it to the British Library and eventually, in 2010, decided to sell it to the library. Hence the remarkable raising of funds.[4]

It is an extraordinary survivor. The only older book known to be in existence and still in its original binding is a Middle Eastern one, a sole representative from one of the many libraries of the ancient world that were destroyed over the centuries in the interests of conquest, retribution, plunder or some version of ever-changing True Faith. The great library of Alexandria, which flourished as a centre of learning from the third century BC, was destroyed four or five hundred years later by the Roman invaders of North Africa, probably in several successive fires. Much of what went up in flames would have been in the form of papyrus scrolls, the precursors to books, and the legend of the library's riches has become a general symbol for lost knowledge.

Bound books are rather hardier than scrolls; no one has yet invented a better storage and retrieval system than the book. Our current digital methods of record are, by comparison, laughably ephemeral, vulnerable to time, error and the obsolescence of technology. Yet from all the pre-Reformation monasteries in Britain that had libraries, the number of books that have survived until today is very small. Duke Humfrey, a son of Henry IV and first Duke of Gloucester, was a learned bibliophile who bequeathed his big collection of books and manuscripts to the University of Oxford when he died in 1447. A hundred years later many of these precious records were dispersed or destroyed by (once again) the Reformation, but enough survived for the library named after him to continue. Yet today, after several more centuries, it contains only three of his original volumes.

The pages of the Gospel from Lindisfarne are made of vellum, calfskin, which is more resistant than paper to the effects of time and damp. Many of the parish records of the sixteenth and seventeenth centuries that still survive owe their continuing existence and legibility to this sturdy material, and to the habit of just-about-literate churchwardens of writing very carefully and clearly. But the vellum manuscripts that were tumbled out of the monasteries at the Reformation were tempting for all sorts of mundane uses. John Aubrey, the commentator of the following century, remarked that 'in my grandfathers' days the manuscripts flew about like butterflies'. The glovers of Malmesbury used them to wrap up kid gloves; housewives used them to line pie-dishes; and the energetic sons of one family known to Aubrey found them just the thing for cleaning guns.

When I remarked this to my British Library friend, he responded that, within his working life, 'seventeenth-century estate maps on vellum were being cut up and sold as lampshades'.

Which, one may wonder, is morally worse in absolute terms: destruction through utilitarian ignorance or deliberate destruction in the name of some ostensibly moral obsession? Girolamo Savonarola's notorious bonfire of books in late-fifteenth-century Florence has become the archetype of the latter sort. But possibly even bleaker is destruction that is merely collateral to a more general obsession. Among the innumerable buildings and their contents destroyed in our own times has been the National Bosnian Library in Sarajevo, burnt by Serbians in 1992. More recently again has been the equally deliberate wrecking by Isis of the Iraqi town of Mosul, including the university, with all its library and records. Along with hundreds of thousands of other books went a ninth-century Qur'an. It seems doubtful whether the obsessed adherents of Isis were aware of this, but one feels that their declared passion for the Qur'an hardly played much of a role in their ill-focused appetite for destruction.

A little while after I had written the paragraphs above, reports appeared in *The Times*[5] and other papers telling of a discovery in St Catherine's Monastery in the Egyptian section of the mountainous Sinai desert, near to where God reputedly revealed the

Ten Commandments to Moses. This Orthodox monastic library, whose origins go back to the sixth century, is one of the world's oldest surviving and contains thousands of manuscripts. The recent presence in the area of an Islamic fundamentalist threat to ancient documents and buildings has been a source of anxiety to scholars around the world, with a close eye kept on it. However, the monks of the ages commonly known as 'dark' were not themselves entirely blameless, regarding the destruction of manuscripts they regarded as heretical or simply without interest.

Vellum, the chosen material for writings, was valuable; new calfskins could not just be sourced at will. So it was a common practice, continuing for centuries, for old writings that had come to be considered less valuable than the material they were written on to be scrubbed off and the surface reused. Lost for ever, you would think, were the earlier inscriptions. But in the 1920s, when the Swiss photographer Frédéric Boissonnas[6] was making an expedition to this ancient fastness to photograph in detail the monks' church, its decorations and treasures, its surrounding mountain views and the monks themselves, he made an odd discovery. When he photographed a page of one of the monastery's most ancient cherished manuscripts, a fourth-century Christian text, he found that his lens revealed traces of 'ghost writing' underneath in a different script. And today the development of multispectral technology, which uses both visible and non-visible light and algorithmic calculations, has been able to re-create and effectively restore some of this material at the monastery. Beneath a Christian Gospel closely written in Syriac Greek were found a design of herbs and instructions in an Arabic script for their use against scorpion-bite, part of what is turning out to be a small medical library, some of it written in languages that are now otherwise extinct. Curing illness – one of the most ancient human preoccupations. After so many centuries, another example of it, recoverable and now recovered.

It is not only written evidence that is retrieved by the burgeoning technologies of the present time. The field of what is now known as bio-archaeology is opening up new possibilities of discovery regarding the distant dead that, even twenty years ago, were quite unattainable. Medieval cesspits have been made to yield up the details of what our ancestors grew and consumed. A human skull, examined with special skill and knowledge, can become the basis for an accurate reconstruction of the face it once bore. Ancient bones, even when fragmented, can reveal not only how that person died, but what sort of age they were, what their health was like earlier, how well or ill they were nourished, what accidents may have befallen them and – most crucially – where, from their DNA, they and their ancestors had their origins. Even more revelatory is dental enamel: where a tooth survives, analysis of its stable isotopes can show not only where the original owner of the tooth spent his or her early years (drinking what water, eating what foods), but where else they lived and at what periods in their life. It can even tell whether the milk on which the person survived in infancy was from a human breast or another source.

> For *everything exists*, wrote William Blake,
> *And not one sigh nor smile nor tear, one hair,*
> *nor particle of dust, not one one can pass away.*

The idea that chronology itself is just one form of perception – that the past is still, in some sense, eternally there and that time is cyclic rather than linear – is a staple of Hinduism. It was believed by the ancient Stoics, by the visionary Blake in the era commonly celebrated as 'enlightened', by Dunne in the twentieth century with his elaborate concept of serial time, and more vaguely by an uncountable number of people around the world today. It is, of course, the basis of innumerable stories of ghosts and hauntings, a very few of them bizarrely well authenticated. It is interesting, to say the least, that a highly precise piece of modern science should now appear to be bringing us one small step nearer to the reality of this human aspiration, to conquer time.

CHAPTER IV

Lost and Found

Cuthbert's book is exceptional in another way from the obvious ones: it has been valued at every stage of its existence. The story of most written documents is far more varied. There is a paradox about old paper, which will haunt this account. Almost any letter, note or list has an immediate value, banally practical or sentimental, to those for whom it has been written, but six months later most have become waste scrap. If this did not happen, if we kept every friendly picture postcard, every laborious note from a child away from home, every letter of condolence, we would all drown in paper. We would also become bogged down in past lives that have lived out their span and should arguably be left in peace. Arguably, too, the sheer act of preserving everything, every *petit papier*, as some American archival institutions have tried to do in the twentieth century, can only lead to devaluation-by-excess. In the same way, the sixteenth-century Spaniards, by bringing so much gold from the New World across the Atlantic, came perilously close to a mass devaluation of the currencies of Europe.

The motives behind the destruction of old letters, bills and the like can range, of course, from the uncaring to the complex and personal. The widow of Captain James Cook, who outlived him by fifty-six years, dying in her nineties, destroyed shortly before her own death all his letters that had made their hazardous way to her when he had been on his world voyages of exploration. Their six children had all died too, most of them long ago, and possibly she felt that life in general had moved so far from the days when she was the young wife of a renowned explorer in a sailing ship that 'no one would be interested in this old stuff any more'. Also, they had been letters to *her*, her one special privilege in a marriage during which Cook was away more than he was present. Rather different was the position of the second wife of Thomas Hardy, who took it upon herself to destroy after his death most of his accumulated letters and papers, the hoard of a whole lifetime, much of which long pre-dated her appearance. It is generally supposed that she knew, or believed, that all this material would reveal matters in the earlier life of this celebrated writer that were best – in her judgement – left unrevealed.

More typically, letters are valued during the lifetime of the original recipients (though sometimes with diminishing enthu- siasm) and discarded by their successors or consigned to some box or attic, which literally becomes an oubliette, a place for things and people to be forgotten. It is then almost entirely a matter of casual chance whether the written material survives for another generation and is perceived by those who come across it as having accrued some extra value or interest, or whether it is finally destroyed. (I exclude from this generalisation such exceptional circumstances as are depicted by Henry James in his novella *The Aspern Papers*. In this, the letters of a famous dead poet, of which the real-life model was Shelley, became a bargaining chip in a contest of wills and ambitions between a woman alone and a would-be biographer, a contest resolved only by the letters' destruction.) All archivists can tell tales of family letters, sometimes hundreds of years old, that appear to have been simply sold off as waste paper, often in the early 1920s, when newly imposed Death Duties were making large ancestral homes financially unsustainable and many of the sons or nephews who should have inherited the accumulated family history were lying in the military cemeteries of the First World War. No wonder, at a certain point, faced with ever-accumulating stacks of yellowed paper, many diminished grand families decided that all these missives from distant, never-known relatives were indeed best used for lighting stoves.

Yet what an enormous mistake they were at the same time making! The very few families, apart from royalty, that have kept collected letters intact over many successive generations stand out as champions of long-term perception. Essentially, in Britain, these were the Paston family, the Verneys and the Stanleys, but each seem to have preserved letters from rather different motives.

The Paston letters, which cover a period from about 1420 to soon after 1500, are the least accessible today to the modern browser, since the English language was still evolving in the fifteenth century, with many local differences: the Norfolk-based Pastons spoke a tongue that was closer to that of Chaucer, in the preceding century, than it was to that of the Elizabethans and Shakespeare in the century to come. But what is remarkable about the pressing missives that the successive John Pastons and Margaret, wife of John I, exchanged with each other and with assorted estate servants and friends is their often baggy, conversational tone: 'And then ... and then ... and I be sure that ... take care that ...' This not the elliptic, Latin-influenced English of the few highly educated men then writing in English – the English that was going to form the vernacular version of the Bible. In Paston communications we hear, across five hundred years, the authentic tone, and even the accent, of people telling life as they currently perceived it, informing, arguing, placating, giving vent to irritation or fear.

Margaret Paston – a redoubtably competent lady in her own right, for all that she had to employ one trusted manservant or another to write the actual words she dictated – might regularly begin her letters, 'Ryght worchypfull hosbond, I recommawnd me to yow, desyryng hertyly to her of yowr wellfar ...' but she would then go on to pour out a description of an argument, of a 'merye' dinner with friends in Norwich, of the progress of a legal suit or of an actual armed attack on their house by someone who laid claim to it. And although she regularly put near the end, 'The blyssyd Trinyte have you in his kepyng', she was quite likely to add afterwards, 'I pray yow trost nott to the sheryve for no fayr langage' or – in a postscript in 1461, five years before her husband's death – 'The pepyll was nevyr bettyr dysposyd to yow than they be at thys owyr. The byll that Howard hathe mad a yens yow and odry hathe set the pepyll in thys contre a rore. God yeve grace it be no werse than it is yet.' The Wars of the Roses were in full force by then and, like many families with an eye to the main chance, the Pastons seem to have avoided an outright support for one side or the other. Yorkist early in the wars, they changed their allegiance on account of a property dispute with the Yorkist Duke of Norfolk (the one whose sheriff was not to be trusted, however fair his language), so the final defeat and killing of the Yorkist king Richard III at Bosworth Field must have been advantageous for them.

The Pastons, for all their energy, do not come across to us as particularly sympathetic. Only in odd moments, such as when a convivial dinner is being described, or when Margaret is asking one of her sons to remember to write to his grandmother, do we get glimpses of action and feeling not bound up in the search for power and wealth, but they were people of their contentious time and those who strived less hard could well end up with nothing. Originally quite a modest family – their name came from the village of Paston, twenty miles north-east of Norwich – the first to start on a socially upward path was John I's father, William Paston, who was born in 1378, became a lawyer, bought land and married well. John I followed the same path: it was through his wife's moderately grand family that he became friends with Sir John Falstaff of Caister Castle near Yarmouth – who should not be entirely confused with Shakespeare's version of Falstaff, which seems to be based, rather, on the Lollard Sir John Oldcastle. John I became Falstaff's main executor and also the inheritor of much of his wealth. Naturally this led to trouble and litigation, and John I was even imprisoned in the Fleet Prison in London for a while, but the family held on to their inheritance. John I, as a lawyer, followed the sensible practice of keeping and carefully filing, along with more formal documents, all the letters that were carried such substantial distances on horseback between London and East Anglia. The habit was continued by his sons – both, rather oddly, christened John. Both got knighthoods; John II died unmarried in 1479 (probably of plague, since that was a year when many died of it), but

John III continued the family tradition of marrying a girl from a rich and influential family, and when he died in 1504 he left the family property well set up.

Subsequent generations do not seem to have had – possibly did not need – the same habit of passionate communication, but the fifteenth-century letters were all kept in the family home. There they remained for another two hundred-odd years, perhaps because they were valued archives, but perhaps from simple inertia. The last direct descendant, William Paston, second Earl of Yarmouth, was a closet Catholic favoured by James II. After James's hasty departure from the throne in 1688, William led a rather chequered career as a Jacobite sympathiser till he died, heavily in debt, in 1732 and the male line became extinct. He had earlier sold some or all of the letters. The name of Francis Blomefield, a well-known antiquarian of the early eighteenth century, is often mentioned as the buyer, but so is that of another antiquarian at that time when the pursuit of the past was for the first time becoming fashionable: Peter le Neve. Le Neve in fact died before Paston did, but his widow seems to have had a good number of the letters, which thus became the property of her second husband. This gentleman did not die till almost forty years after William Paston was gone, and after his death some of the letters seem to have been acquired by a chemist of Diss, a small Norfolk market town. Such is the random fate of documents of whose potential value and interest no one is entirely sure! All one can say is that the letters were then passed on variously from one collector to another, transcripts were made, and at one point doubt was even cast on their authenticity, but fortunately the originals eventually came to light again, in several separate caches. Most are today in the

British Library, though a few are held by the Bodleian in Oxford, at Magdalen College and at Pembroke College in Cambridge.

The letters of the Verney family too begin in the fifteenth century, but the best-known and most extensive run of them, some thirty thousand letters, cover much of the seventeenth century. What with the Civil War, the regicide and Commonwealth, then the collapse of that and the Restoration of the Stuarts to the throne, almost every substantial family in England suffered in some way during one decade or another.

In 1644 the current Sir Ralph Verney, critical of Charles I but a natural Royalist at heart, went to the Continent to avoid capture by Cromwell's men. The family home at Claydon, Buckinghamshire, was sequestered by the parliamentary party for four years. When his wife, making an unobtrusive return trip, managed to get into it again, she wrote to him that it was 'most lamentably furnished, all the linnen is quite worne out … the feather beds that were walled up are much eaten with Ratts'. She died herself in France in 1650, another piece of bad luck for Sir Ralph. Three years later, after an Act of General Pardon had diplomatically been passed, he came home. Two years more and he was arrested again – those running the Commonwealth were becoming jumpy: plots and murmurs were once again in the air. Ralph wrote to his son from the Tower of London that he had been 'brought Prisoner to Towne with divers lords and other persons of qualitty, for we know not what; our own innocence is a Protection that cannot be taken from us …' You might think this over-optimistic, but in fact he seems to have had quite a comfortable and even sociable time while interned, and was let out again after four months. In between these two fugitive periods he had busied himself getting the house back in order, most specifically with plumbing a pipe from a spring. He wrote: 'Perhaps Mr Sergeant at Brill can take the height of it with a Water Levell, my own [spring] too, & I hope they go high enough to come into the Leaden Cisterne in the Water House ...' The pipe he installed was in use well into the twentieth century.

Each generation of Verneys seems to have produced, as well as the occasional misfit or ne'er-do-well, an able member to carry the concept of country-nobility forward in spite of destruction and slaughter. An eighteenth-century Verney followed the classic trend of the time by losing huge sums of money at the gambling table, but he nevertheless rebuilt Claydon with taste and style, and it stands today as a monument to peaceful English living. A nineteenth-century Verney married the sister of Florence Nightingale and encouraged Florence's work on the care of the sick; indeed, he always seemed rather more interested in Florence than in his own wife. There are about four thousand letters at Claydon written by her, though not all of them to Verney himself, for she became a beloved aunt to all the family.

A twentieth-century grandson to that Verney became a successful illustrator, but also carried on the family tradition of record-keeping. He wrote a beguiling book about his experiences as a young man with the army in the Middle East between 1940 and '44, but called the account, with a gesture to the language of his forebears, *Going to the Wars*.

The continuity of family adherence to a tradition of preservation must be almost unique. In 1968, when the current Verney baronet followed on work done by his mother, in summarising the history evident in centuries of correspondence, he noted that the thirty thousand letters from the seventeenth century were still kept at Claydon, along with copious others from later eras. They still are today, under the care of the Claydon House Trust, and are available to visit each month, by appointment.[7]

The Stanley family is always described as 'one of the oldest of the Cheshire families'. A Venetia Stanley, granddaughter of the Earl of Northumberland who was implicated in a Catholic plot against Elizabeth I, became a significant figure in the Stuart court. The chronicler of his contemporaries and their ancestors, John Aubrey, described her as 'a most beautiful desireable Creature', mistress to the Earl of Dorset and probably others, too. She was painted by Van Dyck, married the scientist and adventurer Sir Kenelm Digby and died in mysterious circumstances. There was a disastrous fire at the family home late in the following century, in which many documents were destroyed and maybe – we do not really know – many letters also, but if so, the family made up for this subsequently.

An Edward Stanley, born 1779, the very year of the fire, was an enthusiastic sailor, traveller (and letter-writer) and would probably have liked to be a naval officer. He acquired a degree in mathematics at Cambridge, but learnt no Latin or Greek, oddly for that classics-obsessed period. Nevertheless, being a second son, he was shunted into a convenient Church living. He ended his career as a forthright and liberal-minded Bishop of Norwich, and it was his own eldest son who was allowed to go into the navy. A second son joined a regiment and fought in the Crimean War, from which he returned quite ill. Again the name of Nightingale crops up, for in 1853 this young man's grandmother, Maria Josepha, was writing to her daughter-in-law, the current Lady Stanley, 'I daresay you will hear how Mary [Stanley] & Florence Nightingale are employed in hunting up nurses with a detachment of which Florence is about to set off for Scutari. What an enterprise! ... Nurses must be wanted, but I think the neglect and destitution of the sick & wounded is greatly exaggerated by the Times which delights in ... finding fault.'

The Crimea was the first encounter in which the newly invented telegraph played a part, so it received more coverage than any previous war. Two years later, the same old lady – she was in her eighties – was writing, 'I wish one could talk through an electronic tube, writing is such a fatigue in hot weather.' Her remark was well informed and prophetic: fifty years later she would have become an enthusiastic telephoner.

A second Venetia Stanley, who was no doubt as beautiful and desirable as Sir Kenelm Digby's wife had been, was loved by an early twentieth-century Prime Minister. He pursued her with daily and even twice-daily letters: he was much older than she was and anyway married. This was Herbert Asquith. She kept all his letters, but hers back to him were destroyed. Hardly surprising. An intermarriage with the Mitford family brought the Stanleys into the orbit of Nancy Mitford, novelist and biographer, and it is largely through her that the family letters and memories are now secured from the erosion of time and chance.[8]

The classic trajectory for most letters is from valued record to outdated memento to worthless scrap – then rubbish consigned to oblivion – then, occasionally and selectively, according to circumstances, to reverential recovery. Still, today, a hundred years after the First World War ended, packets of letters from Flanders written in pencil in a muddy trench by some great-great-uncle of whose existence the present generation is barely aware, since he never returned to continue his life, come to light when family homes are cleared. They are often received with pleasure and interest by a museum, local or national. Kept once out of love, hope or grief by the person to whom they were addressed, the letters have been infused by the simple passage of time with a different meaning. By the same token, we do not today stand at war-memorial ceremonies on Armistice Day out of remembrance for known individuals, as people used to do, since all those who knew the dead soldiers of that World War personally are now gone. We attend out of a wider sense of horror at the wanton and pointless slaughter of so many promising lives and in reaffirmation (however ineffective) that it shall not happen again in our time.

Let enough time pass and any written missive from the world that has vanished becomes precious. How glad a museum would now be to receive a medieval shopping or laundry list! And glad they are when some unexpected windfall comes their way. About a dozen years after the beginning of the present century, someone doing repairs to a wall in Corpus Christi College, Oxford, noticed that a tightly folded paper had at some point been stuffed into a crack between stones, presumably to keep out a draught, and had subsequently been plastered and painted over. When the paper was retrieved and deciphered, it turned out to be a fragment of a musical score by Thomas Tallis, complete with words, from a special service held in St Paul's for Henry VIII in 1544, two years before his death. It is known that the service was arranged by Catherine Parr, the final wife who survived the much-married king, and it is thought that the words may be by her. With similar serendipity, two much-folded sheets of paper were found lining the spine of a seventeenth-century book in the printing and publishing archive of Reading University. The sheets had apparently been used to reinforce the binding, and turned out to be from one of the first books printed in England by Caxton's press – a priest's handbook, dating from 1476–7. An interesting example of a printed page being, for once, more significant than a handwritten one.

Papers so unvalued that they are reused for bindings are clearly a fruitful source for lost writings, for in 2018 the Vice-Chancellor of Northumbria University,[9] while rummaging in Cambridge University Library, made a similar find. As part of the backing of another manuscript, and divided into several different scraps, he discovered the score of a lost Christmas carol that had been sung in his own district in the early fifteenth century – 'Parit virgo filium'. So, after five hundred and fifty years, the mute carol proclaiming a virgin bearing a son was given voice again in Newcastle Cathedral.

Not that all paper messages of documentation, instruction or emotion are necessarily in words or musical notation. From the 1920s to the 1980s an east-London shoemaker called Ab Solomons brought his cash wage-packet home to his wife each week in the approved good-husband manner. Only, unlike most husbands, he bothered to enliven the back of the small beige envelope every week with a little pencilled picture – funny, poignant, affectionate, indignant or wry – usually depicting some event, large or tiny, national or personal. He was a natural cartoonist, and over the years the pictures became rather more elaborate and were often augmented with colour.

His wife never said much about these offerings, but she must have valued them, since she kept every single one. Only years after her death did it fall to her great-nephew, a musician and impresario, to rediscover these wordless love-letters and bring them back to a completely new life, in the form of an endearing one-man dramatisation of his family's past times.[10]

A rather similar trajectory to that of letters and other missives is followed by photographs, although the timescale is much shorter. Experiments inducing light to leave an imprint of a leaf or other object were done variously in the 1820s, but it was in 1838 that Louis Daguerre produced a very slowly exposed picture, taken from a high window, of the boulevard du Temple in Paris. An unknown man who happened to be having his shoes cleaned and polished by an indistinct street shoeshine man thus became, by accident, the first ever human to have his picture taken, since he was standing still, leg raised, in one position for many minutes. In the subsequent decade Daguerre perfected his technique and produced little portraits on glass, using silver and mercury, but these works of art had the disadvantage that they were not reproducible. At the same period Henry Fox Talbot in England was producing 'photogenic portraits' by a method that enabled prints to be made and which therefore gradually superseded 'daguerreotypes'. From the 1850s onwards, photographic portraits became generally available and were much in demand – though only for people with enough money to spare for such luxuries.

'Portraits' were what they were. Mother and children, some-times with father too placing a proprietary hand on a shoulder, would be photographed sitting necessarily rigid (because film was still slow) in the photographer's studio, a decor perversely arranged to resemble a bourgeois interior that might be their home. The resultant photos, over the years, would be stuck into a heavyweight album, framed in decorated double-sheets of card, along with other camera portraits of aunts, cousins and nephews. Not till the early twentieth century did photography become significantly faster and cameras more portable, so that informal garden or beach pictures began to fill slimmer albums – but the same fate awaited them. The fact is, if the names of those in each photo are not written clearly beside it, once two generations have passed most of the eternally youthful faces in the pictures are unidentifiable and therefore perceived as not worth keeping. Unlike written material, faces carry little message, once the necessary information that anchors them to us is lost.

Camcorder and video material, those novel delights of the late twentieth century, will probably retain perceived value for longer, though the fragility and vulnerability of such stuff – in comparison with a bound book, or even a simple sheet of paper – means that it will hardly enjoy a long existence, as older forms of record have done. It is the same with early cinema film: the small amount of it that has survived, having by lucky chance avoided being turned into nail-polish or simply obliterated by light and damp, is now prized and expertly remastered. In it, we see people who were dead long before we were born going vigorously about their business and pleasure. Their body-language is like ours, they run and turn as we do, sit on steps, shake their fists, drink things from glasses, push each other, laugh, shoulder heavy weights, drive carts, ancient tractors, trams, prams or tanks. Film of troops during the First World War, especially, has been retrieved and brought back to a semblance of life again recently with a remarkable level of skill and care. Soldiers who, twenty-five years ago, were indistinct, silent black-and-white figures jerking about on old film-stock inappropriately run at modern film speed, can now not only be seen in colour and in their natural movement, but actually heard talking to one another – thanks to artifice and the contribution of professional lip-readers.[11] Touched by their revived appearance and energy, we are inclined to feel these dead men have actually been brought back to life again.

Only, of course, they haven't. They are preserved in an eternal moment that both introduces us to them and alienates them from us. So much about them – their clothes, their weapons, their slang, their bad teeth, their boots, their very way of speaking (if we could hear it for real, which actually we don't) – indicates that it is unmistakably the Past we are viewing. Whereas, several generations ago, people who were inclined to cherish their fore-bears could feel a general sense of empathy that excluded detail of dress, manner or articulation, we do not have that option. Even as we enjoy a privileged view that all the generations before us could not even dream of seeing, we know we cannot reach these people. They are imprisoned in the sheer clarity of their record, disguised in clothes and mannerisms unlike ours, dwellers in a world that is not our own as the frontier of time moves us inexorably further and further from them.

And because the frontier of time, my own time, is the one on which I live and that frontier will presently, for me, in the natural order of things, have run its course, I am not going to discuss the anxiety which preoccupies archivists and historians today: that the arrival of email and of the photo-on-the-phone is even now wiping out vast potential areas of paper record that have been the staple of research for centuries.

Time will show whether this change is just another version of the casually brutal but necessary wastage and winnowing that has always occurred, as described above. Or whether technology itself will overcome its own defects: there is talk of 'saving hard disks'.

In coffins, perhaps? I don't somehow think that in thirteen centuries' time some future archivist will be lovingly cradling a preserved hard disk in his hand and produce the means to decode its secrets.

A better hope is that the sheer ephemerality of the online world will lead (indeed, is perhaps already leading) to a wary revision. The 'paperless office' that was confidently predicted in the 1990s has proved hard to implement. So has the disappearance of the bound and printed book, which was confidently and glumly foretold in about 2010. Let us hope that the paperless future is similarly a chimera.

In addition, it has begun to dawn on populations beguiled by the ease of instantaneous communication that this is, by its very nature, insecure. Impersonation online is seemingly impossible to prevent entirely, and the concept of a 'private email' is something of a contradiction in terms. Those who have a particular reason for wishing to keep their communications discreet (including, it is said, some departments of the Kremlin) are resorting to traditional paper, ink, the firmly sealed envelope and the anonymity of the mass postal service.

Ironically, a far older fear, now lost in time, once focused on the written record itself. In the ancient world, when writing was ceasing to be the preserve of the very few, there were fears that wider literacy would damage the human capacity for memory. Whether this has in fact come to pass, since the general literacy that overtook all developed societies in the second half of the nineteenth century, and the age-old habit of passing on ancient stories orally at the fireside was gradually extinguished, is hard to say. But it is probably true that a brain constantly fed with one-line tweets, invitations to 'like' and the sheer quantity of heterogeneous information now instantly available is not cultivating the habit of memory.

There is, however, one further curious effect of the Internet that researchers are beginning to appreciate. Just as the human memory seems to retain a mass of material that is not readily available but may sometimes reappear under hypnosis, shock, the effects of opioids or simply as the result of a chance encounter or a return to a long-ago place, so a vast body of incoherent individual material is being amassed inconspicuously online. Much of this is untapped, though considerable public anxiety has now built up about the potential misuse of it for commercial or political ends. What has been less remarked is that, just occasionally, by putting unrelated bits of this stuff together, a determined researcher can retrieve a revelatory link.

The unknown person who, in 1941, photographed a group of Polish civilians being executed in mass-reprisal for the killing of one Nazi soldier could not have been aware that among the faces of incidental bystanders he had captured that of a man who would later, and for quite other private reasons, claim he had never been near that town. Nor could this other man dream that, more than sixty years afterwards, the photo might find its way onto an obscure social-media website, and would thus become findable by someone totally unconnected with the event, but with a quite other quest in mind. Such recall of vanished traces has never been possible till now.[12] Everything exists, indeed – potentially.

CHAPTER V

Graven Images

I return to Saint Cuthbert. As a founding father of the Christian Church in the West, he is a popular saint. He has churches all over the United Kingdom, especially in his home territory of the north, though there are several in the London area, too. It so happens that his church in Wells, Somerset, which is England's smallest cathedral city, shelters another remarkable survival from the past, though a piecemeal one.

The role of the 'other church' a few minutes' walk from any great cathedral or abbey cannot be easy. During the upheavals of the seventeenth century Wells was an active centre of Puritanism and many of the saints displayed in niches up the front of the cathedral could hardly have escaped beheading, if they had not already suffered it during the previous century. The nineteenth-century passion for restoration has brought them back to life again. St Cuthbert's did not escape zealous destructiveness, either, though luckily the winged angels that roost up in the cross-timbers of its roof were too high up for Calvinist or Puritan smashing. The medieval reredos in two sections, one on each side of the east wall leading into the choir, was far more accessible. It consisted of men, women and cattle in a series of niches, all going about their lawful pursuits, along with the oxen and donkeys that would have been part of daily life to those who carved them. There was also a camel, with a horse-like face, less familiar occupant of a distant land, which the carvers are unlikely ever to have seen. The skilled men of those times enjoyed creating panoramas of the life they knew with only fleeting or allegorical references to religion, and no doubt the ordinary parishioners enjoyed looking at the results from their seats in the nave, the choir beyond the reredos being for clergy and monks only. In those days such lifelike statuary was tinted bright with colours.

All this medieval life enshrined in stone was deemed unfit to grace a church, probably during the brief reign of Edward VI, Henry VIII's obsessively Protestant teenage son. Men, women and animals had their protruding sections – faces, arms, legs, sickles, spades – hacked off, to flatten the reredos sufficiently for the surface to be plastered over. The bits were stuck in higgledy-piggledy as hardcore to fill the gaps in the niches. A smooth, whitewashed wall was achieved both right and left of the entrance to the chancel, and so it remained for the next four centuries.

Then, sometime in the early decades of the twentieth century, the wall was investigated and the broken fragments were discovered. Unlike all other surviving medieval statuary, their variegated colours were undimmed by time, because the dark in which they had been hidden had preserved them. Yet their resurrection was incomplete. Money, or perhaps enthusiasm, ran out. This was not the cathedral after all. The bits of men and beasts were stored away in crates, while the living tints began to fade a little and many more decades passed. Finally, in 2016, a complete inventory was made of them. What shall happen to them next? The question remains. Could a few of the figures be reconstructed enough to stand again in church? Or is the best that could be achieved some mosaic of disintegration, a respectful and nostalgic gesture towards our lost ancestors? The whole collection has become a paradigm of time's passing: the survival of the past, its inevitable loss and its changing meaning.

In many churches at the Reformation, up and down England, saints and other beloved objects that might be judged too 'Roman' were hustled away, not for destruction but for protection. In a church in Gloucestershire a precious early medieval wooden crucifix was consigned to a hiding place behind wooden panelling, where it eventually disintegrated from damp. When it was rediscovered in the twentieth century, only the head of Christ and one of his feet could be salvaged – thus becoming poignant symbols of the decay of the mortal body which the Christ himself is supposed to have assumed. In a recent time, too, there was found hidden in a niche in the crypt of a church in County Cork, Ireland, a heart-shaped lead box. Inside, there turned out to be the unrecognisably desiccated remains of a human heart – no doubt originally a prized relic. 'The stalk is withered dry, my love:/So will our hearts decay ... '

In a village near Burford, in the Cotswolds, men at work on the foundation for a new church porch in 1861 came upon a small, headless male statue, presumably buried there several centuries before. The men realised that it fitted the empty recess of a one-time shrine in the north aisle of the church, and so placed it there. However, the vicar of the time disapproved, presumably having no sympathy with the high-church movement associated with Oxford that was by then having an increasing influence on Anglican ritual. He told the well-intentioned workmen to destroy the find as an 'idol', and so they dutifully broke it up. Many other parishes could no doubt produce comparable stories.

Other finds have suffered still more destruction than the battered saints or relics, and their eventual rescue has been all the more remarkable. When, in 2015, it was decided to clean out the attics of Westminster Abbey to create a place for a new museum, it was found that the space there between the top of a medieval vaulted ceiling and a floor laid over it around 1700 was full of dust and rubbish. This debris was within a whisker of being swept away when an archaeologist who was present noticed, among the dirt, a myriad tiny shards of broken coloured window glass, and a rapid halt was called to the cleaning. It turned out eventually that they had there some thirty thousand pieces, many of them smaller than fingernails, but which, when put together by a team of specialised restorers in Canterbury, with infinite pains, revealed the remnants of flowers, stars, sun's rays, griffins and saints' faces, the surviving fragments of exquisite workmanship, some of it dating back to the thirteenth century.

One section of the attics, however, offered nothing salvageable. As the archaeologist[13] regretfully remarked: 'The space over the chapels was cleared in the 1950s, and we found it as clean as a whistle, not a dead spider left. Heaven knows what treasures we have lost – but at least what we have done here will serve as a warning to other places not just to bin the lot.'

*

A historian[14] wrote in the 1920s, when after the Great War the sense of the past as a lost country was particularly acute: 'The Memory of the world is not a bright, shining crystal, but a heap of broken fragments ... All history is full of locked doors, and of faint glimpses of things that cannot be reached.'

Even some of the names by which countries are commonly known today are as come-by-chance as if they themselves were broken shards, randomly picked up on the beaches of time. The designation 'America', attached to the whole of a major continent, simply derives from the Italian name of an adventurer who happened to set out from Plymouth to the shores of what became known as New England at the beginning of the sixteenth century, some ten years after Columbus had landed near the same place but believed that he had attained the Far East. The very name 'Britain' is thought to come from the Phoenician word for 'tin', from the days four centuries before Christ when Phoenician sailors from what is now Lebanon and Syria, intrepidly exploring their world, found tin to be mined near the coasts of Cornwall.

Battered or splintered effigies of saints, of biblical personalities, of long-dead bishops and abbots – these scattered remains were, when they were whole, venerated for hundreds of years because they were embodiments of Christian faith and often of very concrete beliefs concerning the power of such figures to intervene in current human existence. In Britain, as in Europe in general, this long era, after near on two thousand years, is drawing to a close. The greatest numbers of practising Christians are no longer to be found in the Western world, but in Africa and the Far

East. Political strife sanctified by religious belief has migrated, too, and typically involves other faiths as well. But even as Christianity has ceased to be, at least for most people in the developed world, a passionate and contentious issue of our own time, it has become an increasingly important vector of the past, a huge coded repository of shared assumption and corporate memory, a sense of belonging to a chain of being far larger than our individual selves.

It has been said that, as concrete Christian faith has declined over the last hundred years, one generation stopped reading the Bible (the main source of literacy for countless ordinary people ever since it was translated into English), but still attended church services regularly. The next generation progressively abandoned the habit of going to church, but retained from their schooldays many of the aphorisms and metaphors of Christian belief and also its moral message. But what of the generations after, largely unexposed to either?

The threatening implication behind this assertion was that once the formulae of the Christian churches was abandoned, the entire message would be abandoned and that a time of heedless, self-centred depravity would set in, an era of home-grown barbarianism. Such was the Nietzschean assumption underlying the cry 'God is dead!' that began to reverberate in cultured circles towards 1900. But there are few signs of this, and abundant evidence that present-day Western society is, if anything, far more aware of the rights and needs of its fellow-human beings than was the case in the past, and more preoccupied with 'truth' and 'fairness' than their great-grandparents were. It does appear that what one might call a Darwinian tendency towards progress is inbuilt in the human psyche, though the perceived nature of progress varies widely from one era or civilisation to another.

Something that has been a matter of pride over a substantial period may find itself demoted by later generations to a target for blame and shame. Imperialism fits into this pattern, as does the enforced conversion dear to generations of believers from Saint Augustine onwards. The long-time Christian practice of trying to impose specific forms of worship, often with great ferocity, whether on fellow-Christians or on 'ignorant heathens' for their own good, is in full retreat. Instead, it is the past, and our ancestors, towards which odium and disapproval are directed. Some of the expressions of this modern moral outrage may seem irritatingly petty – the desire to launder history by destroying the statues of long-dead figures of which present-day mores disapprove is hardly admirable or well informed – but it does undoubtedly point to a continued striving after a set of moral constructs. Those who expressed the fear that, once people stopped believing in the wrath of God they would behave horribly with cheerful abandon, have turned out to be mistaken.

Relatively few people in Western Europe now count themselves as practising Christians, but very many remain cultural Christians, with a huge inherited pack of assumptions about decent, honest and neighbourly behaviour. Food banks for struggling families multiply; town churches open their doors by arrangement on cold nights to the destitute. Crowd-funding efforts for good causes are organised through social media. The desire to Do Good, if necessary at one's own expense, shows absolutely no sign at all of diminishing. It is not, of course, that Christianity has a monopoly on this attitude: it is rather that it has, historically, been a major player.

More specific Christianity has not vanished, but has significantly shifted its mental domain. We visit churches in huge numbers today, and many old and beautiful ones are far better kept and repaired these days than they ever were when supposedly 'everyone went to church', but most visitors are keeping faith not so much with their God as with all the generations lying behind them. We see these fine buildings as great bridges to our own ancestors, our own collective past, and as a means to transcend, for half an hour, the everyday preoccupations that normally crowd our brains. Our general knowledge of the Bible, its stories and its phraseology, may be lamentably defective by the standards of our grandparents, and this is an undoubted loss, but we still light candles and think of others and of our own fate.

In much the same spirit, I have no doubt, the centurion of about AD 400, feeling anxious and preoccupied with multiple cares in his villa on the South Downs, what with the rumours of a possible Roman withdrawal from such outposts of the empire, would make a sunset visit to his household shrine. He was in any case, by that date, probably of mixed Romano-British, Slav or Gallic origins, and may never have actually seen Rome. He was an intelligent man; he knew, with most of his mind, that Juno, Diana, Mercury and the rest of the colourful crew could not really exist in permanence on Mount Olympus in the way men had believed in times gone by. He knew these were written-up stories deriving, perhaps, from some long-ago era that was now distant and done. He had heard of the new Faith that had been adopted by the Emperor Constantine himself, and that this Faith was said to be travelling the sea-lanes and invading men's minds. But he nonetheless derived a sense of relief and of duty accomplished, a few minutes of relaxation after a difficult day, and a kind of insurance for what might be to come, as he stood with hands uplifted before the statue of his favourite god, lit the little lamp and bestowed a wreath of flowers. He was keeping faith with his ancestors and with all that was best in the civilisation that he knew.

But one has to admit that some household gods seem more worthy of physical preservation than others. Partly, as with letters and papers, this depends on their age: a crudely made clay fertility figure unearthed from a Neolithic tomb is not going to be rejected on artistic grounds any more than a medieval Will is going to be condemned as uninteresting because it seems hurried and banal in expression. But the mass-production of inexpensive household gods that came in with the industrial revolution has left all too many figures to uncaring posterity. Some years ago I encountered a whole morgue of them – or perhaps 'a whole geriatric home' would be a better expression, since these enduring images showed no signs of being bundled off to extinction.

We were staying overnight in a moated fourteenth-century castle in central France. The descendants of the family who had owned it for centuries were making great efforts to keep the hugely expensive roofs on the old place by staging summer exhibitions and festivals. We had been invited to a musical recital in its gardens, followed by dinner in its courtyard lit by scores of candles on every available ledge and windowsill, followed – for us – by a hospitable night's stay in one of the castle's many surplus upper rooms. A female cousin of the *châtelaine* showed us to an eyrie furnished with a heavy Victorian bed and a view straight down into the moat worthy of an archery champion staving off the English invaders in the Hundred Years War. The nearest bathroom, she apologised, was two floors down and there might not be enough hot water for a bath, but one could always make *une toilette du chat* at the basin. We agreed that this was perfectly acceptable. Then I asked about the remarkable collection of Virgins, Sacred Hearts and Saints Somebody-or-Other parked in serried ranks on an ugly Victorian sideboard that was crowding the landing outside. The cheerful cousin drooped a little. Oh dear, yes – it was a problem. All these sacred objects had belonged variously to grandmothers, great-aunts and more distant female relatives – the family ran to girls, which had been one of the economic problems that had beset several recent generations – and their owners were now dead and gone. *Quoi faire?* If the family had definitively moved out of the place, no doubt a drastic final solution would have been found for all these objects and much else besides, but as things were … One could not quite throw all these things that had been the recipients of prayers into the moat, could one? Still less chuck them onto a heap of stones at the back of the stables. And just suppose, if one did so, and then something terrible happened …

Just suppose. We entirely saw her point.

But the fact remained, as she clearly perceived herself, that these effigies were in themselves pointless, devoid of rarity, artistic quality or even the accrued value of age. Any value vested in them individually had been extinguished by the deaths of their owners. It has been said that when any person dies, a whole library of memories, knowledge and stories dies along with them, but these saints and virgins were mute for ever; there was no way they could ever divulge the prayers of which they had been the passive recipients, the griefs or resentments that had been poured over them. None of them even appeared to have come from distant shrines, let alone from a more exotic cult. The only possible message they bore was of the narrowness of late-nineteenth-century French provincial piety.

It is a different matter when a small statuette has, in contrast, become an emblem of the wideness of the world and the extraordinary reach of long-ago journeys. One such has come my way – by chance in France, too, but in very different circumstances.

A lifelong Parisian friend had in her flat, along with many books and pictures, a number of ancient objects. Among them was a small ivory Christchild about six inches high. Clearly he had once stood up on a little stand, and his jointed arms may have held a miniature orb and were able to be raised in blessing. But the arms had disappeared from their jointed shoulders and the feet were damaged, too, as if he had been wrenched from the stand. His calm face, delicately carved to look faintly downwards, was untouched, and his hair, slightly curly in a neat bob, retained its red-gold tint. An inconspicuous hole on the crown of his head suggested a missing halo. He spent his days lying on a shelf in front of a row of books, with a small jade sea-creature for company.

I was offered the Christchild as a present and of course I accepted. Apart from anything else, it would have been rude and unkind to refuse him. The current owner had no children and not many satisfactory younger relatives: her numerous friends were mainly gone or very old themselves. When I took the Christchild away with me, it was almost the last time I saw her. Her family origins, of which she had always been rather proud, lay in the Basque Country south of Biarritz: she said the

Child had always been thought to be of Spanish or Portuguese origin, and dating from the seventeenth century.

So he exchanged his Parisian bookshelf for one in London. I would hold him occasionally in my hand, where he fitted nicely, and think what a long time ago the elephant whose tusk he was must have roamed somewhere in north-west Africa. So I knew already that his substance had made one journey, from there to the Hispanic peninsula, but I did not guess this would be only a beginning. My old friend died. Years passed.

Finally I bestirred myself to ask the British Museum if someone could tell me something about the Child. After the customary bureaucratic delay, I was invited to show him to a specialist. Alerted, she had already printed off for me an article entitled 'Marfins no Império Português,'[15] which, I was delighted to discover, included photographs of other Children, with their arms and feet intact, with the same curly hair and the same neat genitals, who might have been twin brothers of my Child.

The specialist agreed that his cultural origins lay in Portugal and that his date might be late seventeenth or early eighteenth century, but thought that he was probably of Indo-Portuguese workmanship from Goa or Macao, those two major Portuguese trading colonies that long pre-dated the British presence in the East. She suggested I talk to another specialist, 'more knowledge-able than I am', at the Victoria and Albert Museum, and thus it was that I discovered the extraordinary journeys that my Child seemed to have made. From being a one-time incarnation of God, he has become, for me, an incarnation and precious testimony of the extraordinary extent of both Christian proselytising and of trade routes in an era when ships were very small and precarious, sailed by the sun and wind, and when many sailors were still half-afraid that they might disappear off the end of the Earth.

The second specialist[16] thought that my Child was probably carved in the Philippines, still further east than Macao, though possibly by a Chinese craftsman. Was he then, I wondered, of Indian elephant ivory? No, he was African: the raw ivory of elephants' tusks had been imported overland from Africa to the Persian Gulf and thence across the Indian Ocean, well before the Portuguese and Spanish missionaries and conquerors turned up in the Far East seeking 'Christian souls and spices' following Vasco da Gama's epic journey of discovery at the end of the fifteenth century. By the time that Spain had conquered the Philippines, the best part of seventy years after da Gama, the skills of local Filipino and Chinese craftsmen with ivory were well recognised in Europe, for they had long been makers of ivory chopsticks and fans. It seems that at that time the little figures they also carved were secular rather than religious. A local merchant remarked disapprovingly in 1592 that the ivory was 'carved into human forms, the workmanship of which is fine and artful; however, one cannot put them anywhere, or give them as a decent present'. Evidently others besides him had noticed this inconvenient and possibly scandalous fact, for from then onwards there seems to have been a remarkable production of acceptably holy figurines, for markets both in Europe and in the recently and forcibly Christianised New World in the Americas. They thus became the bearers, these small statues, of an historical and cultural significance far beyond the conceptions of those who pragmatically carved them.

It may be that the Child was brought back from the Philippines to the lands of his cultural genesis on the long route through the South China Seas and the Indian Ocean, the Gulf of Hormuz and Arabia, overland where the Suez Canal would eventually run, and so through the Mediterranean to Spain. But there is a probability that he made an even longer voyage. Keen to make money out of what they rightly perceived was an expanding market for religious artefacts in both Mexico and Peru, the Philippine merchants took to sending heavily laden ships known as 'Manila galleons' all the way across the Pacific to Acapulco on the western Mexican coast. These carried religious sculptures, along with such other prized goods as porcelain, jewellery, decorative glass beads, silks – and the universally required spices. Some sculptures were sold in Mexico, paid for with silver mined locally by the Spanish invaders, and would in time have made their way north to the newly established monasteries of California; others were carried further down the coast to Peru.

And there is a further probability, for some of the little statues are known to have been taken across Mexico by land to Veracruz, the port of its eastern coast, and thence shipped out of the Gulf of Mexico, round the tip of Florida, over the Sargasso Sea and so right across the Atlantic to land at last on the Hispanic peninsula, in Portugal or northern Spain. If the Child took that route, the conclusion is that, first as raw ivory and then in his finished, expertly crafted state, he circumnavigated the entire globe before fetching up in his cultural homeland, in the peace of some pious household or convent. And it may even have been back home, before he reached his settled destination, that the final touches of colour were put on: the tints of his calm lips and eyes, the red-gold of his hair.

But peace was not for ever. It is clear that at some point in the next several hundred years he suffered some terrible damaging event – private fit of anger or rejection? Public anti-religious assault? Who can say, except that whatever it was seems to have long pre-dated the destruction of religious objects in the Spanish Civil War of the 1930s, since by that time he was lodged safely in Biarritz, over the French border. It was after the Second World War that my friend took him to Paris as a family memento, when living family ties with the Basque Country were coming to an end.

The Child has, however, been lucky to survive so long, even in a battered and partial state. Many of his contemporaries did not make the journey back to Europe. The Manila galleons were notorious for being overloaded and unwieldy and a number of them are known to have sunk on the long, perilous journey towards the Mexican shore. The *Santa Margarita* went down in 1601, on the rocks off a cluster of Pacific islands, after having been already eight months at sea and almost 1,500 miles from the Philippine shores. Her loss was recorded at the time, but not till the end of the twentieth century did it become possible to locate the wreck and excavate it properly. When this was done, among the many precious objects brought to the surface were small-scale ivory statues that (once again) might have been brothers of my particular Child. Many were undamaged, except that any coloured tints had been bleached from them and the effect of almost four hundred years of salt water had been to make the ivory surface slightly sugary, 'more like alabaster', said those whose handled it.

The real importance of this shipwrecked treasure has been that it has enabled historians to suggest dates for certain types of statue much earlier than had been supposed. It had been usual to date figures such as the Child to the end of the seventeenth or the first half of the eighteenth century, when they were almost mass-produced. But the fact that the *Margarita* is known to have gone down in 1601 is clear evidence that the models found on her were extant right at the beginning of the seventeenth century, only a few years after the Philippine merchant had been complaining that the human forms produced by the indigenous craftsmen were 'not decent'. Even if it took months, and the constant risk of death, to traverse the great seas, the international trade of the time was clearly highly responsive to demand. The Child may be even older than my French friend thought he was. And far more cosmopolitan.

CHAPTER VI

Trees Last Longer than People

The Virgins and saints evacuated to the topmost floor of a medieval castle seemed bereft of all their meaning; the Christchild who has travelled so far has been transmogrified into a bearer of historical and geographic significance far beyond the concepts of the unknown artisan who carved him on the other side of the world. In contrast, another Virgin I feel that I know, definitely French, this one, has survived in her original form and setting, together with a precious scrap of her personal history that is still just about preserved.

Over forty years ago, I and my family bought a very small but solid stone house on the edge of a village in central France, in the area commonly called by its old name, the Berry. Readers of my *Célestine, Voices from a French Village*[17] will be familiar with this village. I wrote about it in that book as a specific place but also, it transpired, as every-village, everyone's memory of a rural childhood, of distant grandparents, of 'the old country', for American and Antipodean readers. The Voices were principally letters written a century and a half ago to a girl called

Célestine, which long after her death were, by a happy chance, destined to save her name from the common oblivion. But for the moment I am concerned with the Virgin in the Wood – *la Dame dans le bois*, as she is called.

There are still many small woods near the village, the remains of the great forests that once enveloped this fertile part of France. Oak and ash grow in abundance, as do Spanish chestnuts, *chataignes*; many of these must have been planted on purpose, since chestnuts were for centuries a staple of the peasant diet in the colder, leaner months of the year. The copse that encircles the back-lane to the Big House of the village is indeed called *le Bois de Chataignes*, but the part of it that continues on the far side of another small road has come to be called *le Bois de la Dame*. It was only several years after we acquired our house that, going exploring, we realised why the wood was so named, for the Lady was well hidden. Bracken and brambles grew high, almost submerging a vestigial footpath. It was evident that, by the late twentieth century, only a few people came there.

Years later, I wrote:

… a small iron Virgin with a Child in her arms stands on a stone plinth in the recess formed by three tall trees. She is a typical statuette of the second half of the nineteenth century; her pretty, impassive face is commonplace, but her lonely situation invests her with a certain austere power. I have visited her at all seasons: in summer when the woods are green and gold and alive with woodpeckers; on a day in deep winter when the hoar-frost on a spider's web made a breathtaking lace veil against her iron cheek; and again in very early spring when the whole bare wood above the carpet of dead leaves was suffused with a blue, expectant light.

For a long time I assumed that her presence was due to some ancient, pagan cult in this wood. My guess was that the Family of the Big House, whose material success in local iron forges in the early nineteenth century had been transformed into land-owning benevolence and setting-a-good-example, had decided that all this Berry folk-stuff about wood-nymphs and fairies and witches and night-time Beasts must be respectably Christianised. I knew that, together with an enthusiastic village curé, they had caused assorted crucifixes to be placed at crossroads, presumably to eradicate the memory of haunted gibbets or other undesirable associations. My theory seemed to be supported by the current head of the Family, a lady in her eighties, who had me to tea in her drawing room, which was full of pretty and valuable things. She said she had always understood that the Lady in the Wood had been placed there in memory of a young wife, the grand-mother she had never known, who had died having her one and only son – the man from whom the now-extensive Family were all descended.

I was not quite sure she was right, for in that case surely the plinth would have carried some inscription, and I knew there was none. But I naturally did not say so.

An elderly farmer, whose unschooled intelligence and reten-tive memory were an enduring source of pleasure and interest to me, produced a different origin for the Lady, one whose specific nature seemed to resonate more with what my own researches were telling me. His grandfather, he said, had told him that the statue had been put there in memory of a child who had been killed in an accident near that spot, a boy who had been climbing a tree after a magpie's nest and had fallen and broken his neck.

But that could not have been an ordinary village boy? A statue on a plinth was an expensive memorial.

No, not just any boy. He was in some way connected with the Big House. Not exactly one of the Family, no. But the head of the Family of the time was his guardian, or some such.

The statue dates from sometime in the second half of the nineteenth century. I knew from my own research that the death in childbirth that it supposedly commemorated had taken place in the early 1860s. I also knew that the bereaved father had felt unable to marry again – ostensibly because he could not forget his beloved young wife, but more probably because French laws of inheritance would have made a remarriage financially and socially disastrous for him. He was himself the son of a tradesman in the local market town who had made money selling linen sheets through a network of pedlars. It was by marrying the only daughter of an ironmaster-turned-landowner that this young man had acquired the status and occupation of a landed gentleman. On this wife's death, his widowed mother-in-law had moved into the Big House with him to care for the motherless boy; his own position in society depended upon him continuing to run the estate that was now legally the property of his son rather than himself. If he had married again, and doubtless had more children, this would have compromised his whole position as trustee of his son's possessions.

When his wife died he was an active, handsome, intelligent man of barely thirty. His first name was Victor, a suitable one for a man who had made good by marrying 'up', and who had every intention of maintaining and enhancing his position in the world of rural, conservative France. It would have been too much to expect that he should lead, henceforth, a celibate life, but this simple fact could not, of course, be mentioned aloud or even thought about: his only son was being reared by the grandmother in passionately literal Catholic belief. So Victor made sure that he retained a number of unspecified business interests in the market town where he had grown up, and also in the county town some thirty-five kilometres away. It was generally recognised that these interests often required his attendance in one town or another, sometimes overnight ... Later, when his son was sent to a Jesuit boarding school in Poitiers, the grandmother accompanied the boy there to ensure that his delicate health was properly looked after. Victor was then able to revert to a more bachelor life and spent much of each winter away in town.

'Of course he did not spend all his time alone, and I'm sure we have a number of second and third cousins scattered about the locality that we don't know about!' a legitimate great-grandson of Victor once remarked to me cheerfully. He too was a good Catholic and proud to be a member of the distinguished local Family, but he did not share the reverence for his sainted ancestors shown by his aunt in the Big House.

The most likely explanation for the Lady in the Wood would seem to me that there was indeed a boy who died there in a fall, and that he was Victor's 'ward' (*pupille*), as children of uncertain origin were commonly described at that time. Perhaps Victor gave his mother-in-law to understand that the boy, from the local town, came of very respectable tradespeople, that his father was dead and that he was a bright boy in whom Victor was taking a benevolent interest ... Perhaps she really believed him or perhaps she did not. But likely she too had taken to the boy, a nice, younger holiday companion for the cherished only son, and they all grieved for him when he had his terrible accident. Whatever the exact truth, it was not an ordinary peasant boy who had his own shrine erected after death.

Each time we returned to spend some time in our house I made a point of visiting the Lady. When the banks and ditches by the roadside were filled year after year with spring cowslips, I would bring her a bunch and ask her to keep those dear to me safe, not quite sure to what aspect of her complex presence I was paying my respects.

One year, after a particularly hard winter, I noticed that the rougher ironwork at her back was beginning to corrode with frost and rain. During a hot summer spell on my next visit I bought a small pot of anti-rust solution and painted her with it all over. It gave her iron surface a pleasant, faintly silvery sheen. I never knew if anyone noticed. I think the *garde champêtre* may have, since he is the local employee whose job it is to keep an eye on blocked ditches, dangerous branches and the like, but if he did, he perhaps assumed it to be the handiwork of someone from the Big House, in whose ownership the wood lay.

Years later again, finding the path to the Lady was made almost impassable by a particularly fine crop of blackberries, I mentioned this fact at the Big House. The elegant old lady who had told me the statue was for a dead young mother was no more: her daughter had now assumed the role of guardian of the Family story. She thanked me, pleased with my interest, and said that she would give orders that the path should be cleared.

It is several years now since I visited the Lady, motionless for ever with her chubby iron babe upheld in her arms. I doubt if anyone else brings her flowers – or will renew the anti-rust treatment – and I feel a momentary pang. This is probably less for the statue herself than for what she represents of permanence and endurance in a place where, during forty years, I assiduously cultivated an alternative French life that I have finally laid aside.

To leave somewhere where you have put down roots, however seasonal, where known mugs and plates and saucepans are waiting for you each time you arrive, where favourite books and CDs will come to life again, where jeans and spare jerseys and cushions are ready to be revived from a moth-proof chest – where furniture that you have made yourselves is quietly ready to be repossessed and where tins bought providentially months ago to provide a first-night supper are waiting in the cupboard – where wood is ready by the stove that only needs to be lit, and a long-ago wren's nest is still there preserved on the high mantelshelf ... is a definitive step. To give away or abandon all this paraphernalia of life, however simple, requires a degree of resolution. To leave a place you have come to know intimately, where you greet and are greeted by everyone en route to the baker's and by the owners of stalls at the weekly market in the town – somewhere you arrive each time thinking, 'I must go and see old Madame Chose ... And we really ought to invite Les Alabrys du Besoin to a meal ...' – to say a final goodbye to all this busy life, constructed over many years, is hard. Inevitably, when we make up our minds to do so, having spent several years preparing ourselves and mentioning this decision to our slightly disbelieving French friends and neighbours, it comes to feel like a partial rehearsal for a much more fundamental departure. '*We brought nothing into this world, and it is certain that we can carry nothing out ...*'

It may, of course, be quite useful to have such a rehearsal. You find out you can actually do it.

'But how,' one friend asked me, 'can you bear to leave a place that has been so important to you – and you to us – a place you have written about, have really put on the map?'

I had wondered that myself for a while. But gradually I came to realise that it was precisely because I had invested so much, mentally and emotionally, in this small patch of France that I had come to feel that my life there was in some sense completed. By my research and the publication and success of my book, *Célestine*, in French as well as English, I knew that I had in a sense given people's own fugitive pasts back to them, and that whole rewarding experience was to me now completed. Time had, in its inexorable way, moved on. Most of my valued inform-ants, who had vouchsafed to me their memories of childhood and youth, and scraps of information about more distant and dead inhabitants, were now lying in the village cemetery them-selves. I had been so lucky to have known them.

Our house too, originally a wonderful place for us to create an alternative French existence, had come to the end of its cycle with us. We had extended it with our own hands, learning as we went along how to mix cement, lay a breezeblock wall, render it, and even how to construct and tile a roof. We had insulated the main roof timbers, cleaned and lit the attic, installed a kitchen sink and organised plumbing, constructed kitchen surfaces, shelves and beds, rejoiced in the wood-burning stove, hung pretty curtains over storage spaces, added cushions and pictures. We had created an idyllic farm-kitchen sort of place in which we entertained people of all kinds. But we knew really (even if our guests, lulled with good food and drink, did not perceive it) that this was still in essence a small, primitive abode, where mice roamed freely for much of the year and where the cold struck up through the battered and cracked red floor tiles that were laid straight over the earth of France.

What we had in fact made, without consciously planning it, was a French version of the rural world of our own youth and of the vanishing generation we had known in our first decades in the village, the 1970s. In those years a few horses still clopped in front of carts, and an old man scattered seeds methodically in his field by hand, an archetypal figure going forth to sow. We ourselves had each, for different personal reasons, emerged from backgrounds that could not, in adult life, offer us much emotional support or sense of continuity. The small house was our stake in a past we had hardly known intimately, but had respected and cherished. Never wanting to transform the place too far from its ancient origins, we had not put in central heating, let alone rebuilt the walls to insert a damp-course. We had no television reception or wi-fi, and no comfortable stuffed armchairs. In short, it was not a place for an ageing couple to spend much time, and the younger generation themselves found it too uncomfortable and primitive. We were tired of the responsibility of it. And just physically tired. Friendly local neighbours were eager to take the house on, as an extension for their burgeoning family empire. They would make modern alterations. With them, we knew that the place would have a further incarnation.

Houses can go through many cycles, for their lives are commonly much longer than ours. My last act of love and effort for the place was to research the house's own history, something I had not done when I was re-creating the lives of Célestine and those connected with her, for Célestine had lived on the other side of the village. So, on our very last visit, when we were saying our goodbyes, I was able to give people as a final present a booklet in French recounting what I had found out about the lives of those who had built our small house – longer ago than most of the houses in the centre of the village.

They had been poor, that distant family who had lived in our spaces, walked beneath our lintels, turned the heavy old key in our lock, warmed themselves at our hearth, poor even by the modest subsistence standards of pre-industrial rural life. But they had the courage, sometime before the French Revolution of 1789, to raise this house on a scrap of land beside a path – to raise it with their own hands, with goodness knows how much evening-and-Sunday endeavour. Men already tired from long, back-breaking days of labour in more prosperous men's fields would have dug foundations with a pick, as we did, fetched heavy loads of stones and lime too from somewhere else in a borrowed cart, sawed timbers, called on neighbours, as we did, to help raise a roof beam – drunk a triumphant glass of wine to the fact, as dark was rapidly coming down and their weary womenfolk, worn out themselves from collecting bracken and furze to thatch the roof, were desperate to get the evening soup on the table.

Both I and those who received my account were pleased that another handful of such people had been brought back from the quiet darkness of forgetting.

A stout old oak tree on the other side of the road must have been a slim young one by an unmade packhorse route when it saw the house go up. There was a plan about thirty years ago to cut it down – 'for firewood', was the feebly traditional reason given – a plan fervently opposed by us and fortunately by the owner of the

Big House as well. It is now secure from such depredation. At much the same time two other sapling oaks had inconspicuously planted themselves at different points in the hedges round our garden. Should he remove them, our elderly farming neighbour asked? He could do it now, but soon they would get too big to shift easily. No, no, please leave them, we said. We'd like them there.

Today, they are tall and fine: another couple of hundred years and they will, with luck, be massive, valued veterans themselves. They are our silent monument.

Of course we still get news from the village. One day in April 2015 it was of a dramatic and tragic kind. A young girl of the Family, a granddaughter of the present old lady, had been on a holiday trip with her fiancé on the far side of the world, in Kathmandu. (Concepts of appropriate Catholic-girl behaviour have been much modified over the last generation, even in its French heartlands.) When a violent earthquake hit the city and many buildings collapsed, she and the young man just happened to be visiting the top of the ancient Dharahara Tower in the city centre. Most of the tower crashed to the ground. They were the only French tourists to die in the capital that day.

She was in the direct line of descent from the young wife of Victor. That girl dead in childbirth must, I calculate, have been her three-times great-grandmother. I think of both of them, and of the unknown boy who died falling from a high tree where he, too, was enjoying himself and looking forward to a whole life stretching ahead.

And I think, too, of the wren's nest that sat for many years, preserved, high up on our mantelshelf. It was recovered, empty, from a bush one summer, by another young girl who had the happy idea of 'mending it – for next year's wrens'. Our son loved her; she was eminently lovable. But by the time the wrens were nesting the following year, she had been brutally killed.

There are occasions when an evil that we would like to believe belongs to a bygone era, or to a distant and barbaric part of the world, devastates the edifice of protection and achievement that we have built around ourselves and those we hold dear, and there is no comfort to be had, no answer. *La mort nous parle d'une voix profonde mais pour ne rien dire.*

CHAPTER VII

Letters to Célestine

The tale of Célestine's letters is a perfect example of a small bunch of obscure papers whose survival is almost random, and whose initial 'discovery' seems less a discovery than a mild surprise, but which turns out eventually to have a transformative effect not only on the life of the finder, but on the collective memory of a community and of others in the world beyond it.

I refer to them in brief as 'Célestine's letters', but they were written *to* her. They were all but one love-letters, or at any rate proposals of marriage, penned between 1863 and '64 when she was nineteen and twenty, plus one from an errant younger brother dating from ten years later.

Marie-Célestine was the daughter of the village innkeeper, a man from a family that had traditionally been weavers. That had been a good and even prestigious occupation in the long, little-documented centuries when almost all the clothes worn by the French peasantry were made of locally produced linen and wool; but by the time of Célestine's birth in 1844 the trade of weaving was in precipitous decline. The industrial revolution, so long delayed and partial in comparison with the same phenomenon in Britain, was at last beginning to have its effect even in the rural heartlands of central France. At the same time roads navigable by carts and even coaches were at last coming to penetrate the oak forests and trackless heaths that lay between one village and another. In setting up the inn in about 1840 in the old family house by the village church, Célestine's father, Silvain-Germain Chaumette, was showing shrewd intelligence. He had also, somewhere along the line, learnt to read and write, a skill not shared at that point by many of the worthies who sat on the village council and whose minutes he kept. Research has also revealed that when the first school was opened in the village he, unlike most of his neighbours, sent his daughter to it as well as his two sons.

So Célestine Chaumette, growing up as an innkeeper's daughter in a world that was on the cusp of change, was a desirable prize for an enterprising local boy. At least six of them tried their luck with her in the space of twenty months, with highly honourable written proposals of marriage that in most cases indicated fervent emotion as well. However, the man she actually married, rather suddenly when she was not yet twenty-one, left no epistolary trace, or none that she kept. His family were nut-oil producers, which was, like weaving, a declining trade. Presumably her parents approved of him, since the great concern of several of her other suitors was that Silvain-Germain Chaumette might not think them adequate as a son-in-law.

Célestine seems to have been docile and sweet-natured: people who, as youngsters, had known her in her old age or by reputation, described her as *gentille*, kind and correct, with a tactful way of dealing with inn customers whom she judged to have drunk enough. She was also, one must suppose, slender and pretty as a girl. Photography was not an option for the rural French of the nineteenth century, so there is no picture of her when young. However, some time after my book based upon 'her' letters had been published in a French edition, and she was launched on her strange path to becoming a retrospective celebrity, I was given two photographs of her with other people, both said to have been taken in 1911 by a village curé. She would then have been sixty-seven years old, and wore the traditional local cap, with a white bow under the chin, that was still standard for mature ladies, though the following generation had by then abandoned this becoming dress.

In one picture she is sitting, posed in a chair, with her son, daughter-in-law and a young inn maidservant standing around her, but though she is looking obediently at the camera, she is stretching out a friendly hand to a large dog sitting beside her. In the other, a small, informal snapshot, she is on the steps of what had for the past thirty years been her own inn, with an apron on and a crock of something (honey?) in her lap. A little girl with a just-visible kitten in her arms sits beside her. What have been identified for me as her husband, Pierre Robin, and two neighbours are there, plus four unidentifiable women who, from the fact that they are all wearing the large hats of the time, must have been visitors. A cheerful Sunday occasion? I hope so.

In fact 1911 was the year the Chaumette-Robin inn and a number of bits of land they owned around the village had to be sold. The inn, once so prosperous, 'the best inn to the south of La Châtre [the nearby market town] for miles around', people said, was failing. There were two other, more competently run establishments in the village now. Célestine, who had inherited the place from her parents, had done her best and had 'set the tone' there. The only son of the marriage, Charles, had been sent successfully on a cookery course, and for some time all went well. A room for dances was even built on at the back of the old house. Charles, however, according to one of my elderly informants who remembered him from her childhood, was 'as lazy as a dormouse', an impractical dreamer. He was also – like his father – over-fond of a drink, the classic weakness of the pub-keeper. He was married off to a suitable girl whose family had some genteel standing in the district. However, this girl, Blanche, went into an apparently manic state after the birth of their only child and seems never fully to have recovered her equilibrium. When people began avoiding the Chaumette-Robin inn because they found her so odd, its failure was inevitable.

After the sale, Célestine and her husband, who was well into his seventies by then, left the village to live in a narrow old street in La Châtre; he still had family in the town. His death was recorded there three years later, in November 1914. There was fierce fighting in Flanders by then: people had other, more obviously tragic deaths on their minds.

Célestine herself lived on almost another twenty years. And, true to form as a once-pretty and sought-after girl, she does not seem to have been entirely alone. She had, I was told, 'a friend' in La Châtre who lived nearby. The word my informant used for this person was *bon ami*, the traditional term for a companion-lover: she at once corrected herself, but the general message was clear – 'Of course I don't mean … They were both old people by then, and anyway he was the retired curé from Crevant, just down the road! But he was her special friend and they spent their days together.'

The person who told me that is now, like almost everyone I knew in the first twenty-five years of our presence in the village, dead herself. The last personal memories of Célestine have slipped, as nearly all memories must, into the quiet dark. There is nothing in this brief outline I have given of Célestine's life, its setting and its time, to suggest that she might one day live again in the perceptions of strangers, and in the imaginations of people far from her in every sense. Yet she has.

In her long life she would, as the daughter of an innkeeper and later an innkeeper herself, have known or been known to some hundreds of people. This was already much more contact than was the lot of most peasant girls, stuck on the family farm, often with little choice but to marry the boy whose family owned an adjoining field or two. But today, since my account of her life has made its way out into the world, in various editions and languages, Célestine is known to thousands upon thousands of people, many of them in lands such as America and South Africa of which she could only vaguely have heard and in others, such as Australia and New Zealand, of which she may hardly have been aware at all.

I never expected the book to travel so far, and nor did its not-entirely-enthusiastic English publishers. Yet travel it has, and continues to do so, twenty-five years now after its first appearance. I have received scores of letters about it. Readers in the United States, with family names varying from Chaumette to Shumacht, have wistfully claimed descent from Célestine, although it is clear from my account that her sole direct descendant, a granddaughter, never had children. Other readers, more realistically, have simply written to thank me for a book that has recalled for them their own grandparents' stories of a vanished European past and made them realise how rich in experience this past had been. It gradually became evident to me that Célestine had, without my planning it, become an ambassador for the world we have lost.

It is as if the letters written to her in the 1860s have, through the alchemy of time, changed their nature. Love-letters are, at the outset, entirely private, personal and frequently – in spite of the conviction of permanence typically expressed by their writers – as ephemeral as butterflies. The passion they declare is either transformed later into something less fragile or fades away. If the letters are still kept, then it is for comfort, pride, nostalgia or regret: they have become messages from a youthful time now gone. But the appearance of these particular, obscure letters in a book some hundred and forty years later has made them into messages of another sort. They are precious historical documents, and finally their brave claims of 'true for ever' have been realised in a way in which their writers could never have dreamt.

In the first chapter of *Voices from a French Village* I explain that I found the letters when I happened to be collecting a small embroidered footstool from an otherwise emptied village house. I did not go into detail of why this took place, because the odd combination of circumstances did not seem relevant to the story of Célestine herself that I had embarked upon telling. But today the sheer chain of coincidences, and possibly a moral message underlying them, seems to me part of the whole wider story of

Célestine Chaumette's obscure existence, the legacy both familial and personal that she left behind, and her extraordinary posthumous destiny.

The old gentleman who had been the last occupant of the small house where I found the letters was a painter with a British name, Norman Lloyd. He had been born in Australia, probably not long after 1890, we calculated, since he was over eighty when we first got to know him in the village in central France in the early 1970s. 'You must meet him,' villagers said to us. 'It would be nice for you.' We were inclined to disregard this: we had not bought a cottage in France to associate with other English-speakers. But by and by it dawned on us that what these kind people meant was that it would be nice for Norman Lloyd – 'Monsieur Norman', as they all called him, the double-l of his surname defeating them. Sure enough, we did soon meet him, painting away in oils on fine days in corners of the parish, in a style generally characterisable as Post-Impressionist. He invited us to his house to see other examples of his work: some of it seemed a little routine (he was, after all, an old man), but some we liked a lot.

He was alone in the house these days. His earliest contact with France, he told us, had been as a soldier in the First World War, in 1916. We understood that he had been wounded in that war, though not to any lasting ill-effect. Sent to convalesce in England, he stayed there afterwards, married an Englishwoman and lived in St John's Wood, which between the wars was an inexpensive, slightly arty area of north London. He seemed to have retained an interest in France and contacts there, presumably through his painting. He was elected to the Royal Academy of Arts. He was apparently back in France late in the Second

World War; at any rate he was in Paris after the Liberation of 1944, in what was described to me by a villager as 'a liaison job'. This can hardly have involved much linguistic skill, since his French had been learnt entirely by ear and was always rudimentary. However, it was said to have been during this period in Paris that he met, 'in bohemian circles', a lady, no longer young herself any more than he was, with whom he formed a lasting attachment that was to shape the course and setting of the rest of his life. This was Marie-Zénaide Robin, daughter of Charles Robin and his unstable wife Blanche, and only grandchild of Célestine.

Zénaide (as she was always known) had been born in 1895, so by 1944 she was approaching fifty. She had had, for all her adult life, a secretarial or clerking job in Paris in the huge maw of the French civil service that is known collectively as The Administration. She had been living for many years in a little flat overlooking the place Dauphine on the tip of the Ile de la Cité by the Pont Neuf. Such a central, desirable location would cost a fortune to rent today, but those were other times. Paris, a haven of fixed rents, was then a city of resilient poverty in which someone with a steady job and without grand ideas could live very comfortably, even taking regular meals out in one of the innumerable family-run restaurants. Zénaide was described to me by someone who had known her well as a 'person out of the ordinary, kind, warm, open-minded … Not really a good-wife-and-mother type, more of an intellectual. Someone whom people remembered.' Displaying an artistic bent that seems to have been remarkably advanced for the times, she decorated her eyrie with pieces of antique furniture picked up in flea-markets and with little patterns of mirror-glass set into plaster. She also dyed her hair.

In 1931 her grandmother Célestine, who had effectively brought her up and to whom Zénaide was more attached than to her unsatisfactory parents, breathed her last, aged eighty-seven, in a home run by nuns. Within two years the parents themselves were both dead, leaving to Zénaide the small house in the village that was full of the furniture and possessions, the linen and china and embroidered chair-covers, that the family had acquired at the inn in the prosperous days when it must have seemed for a while that a decent bourgeois status was being attained. A few of these items must have gone into exile in La Châtre with Célestine and her husband and eventually come back to the village. Did the letters travel back unlooked-at in the drawer of some piece of furniture, I wonder? Or did Célestine take them with her to the nuns' home along with her clothes, her missal and the few family photos from prosperous times – the last cherished belongings? Either way, the letters, which were packed tightly into one of the small cardboard cases in which pious families then kept baptism and First Communion cards, found their unobtrusive way back to the village to which they had originally been sent almost seventy years before.

Once her parents were gone, Zénaide made the small house in Chassignolles her holiday home. Over the years she was accompanied there by several different gentlemen at different times. She never married. She was of the generation in which so many potential husbands had died in the killing fields of the First World War, but I am not sure she really wanted to marry anyway. It was to this same house, fortunately then in the Free Zone south of the Loire, that she retreated from Paris in 1940 when, along with other Parisians, she fled the approaching Germans. This time she brought with her a little girl, characterised by some as a 'refugee', of which there were many in the area, but also reputed to be the daughter of Zénaide's current 'gentleman friend ... He was a foreign gentleman. Not a native French speaker, no.' What became of that friend is unknown, but whatever the course of Zénaide's subsequent moves in the war, the child survived. For one day, about forty-five years later, the village *mairie* received a visit from a lady 'of a certain age, very well dressed', according to the Secretary. When she mentioned this visit to me, she added, 'I don't know quite how to describe the lady to you. Not like anyone from round here ...' I surmised that what she meant was 'very Jewish-looking', but that she thought it might not be quite polite to say so.

This lady explained that she had stayed in the village as a young child. Passing through the area now with her husband, she hoped to find again the house, which she could only locate by describing its owner – 'Zéna, I called her. A wonderful person, so kind and such fun ... I really have a golden memory of those months.' So it would seem evident that Zénaide was one of those largely anonymous French citizens to whom a number of France's Jewish children owed their lives. Indeed, Norman Lloyd, in old age, used to tell a garbled story of Zénaide having carried a number of refugee children off into the safety of the woods, when the Germans were visiting retribution on central France after the Normandy landings of 1944.

In the twelve years between the end of the war in Europe and the mid-1950s when Zénaide died, she and Norman apparently made a habit of spending July and August together in her small village house. Indeed, I get the impression they spent whole summers there, once she had retired from her job. How this was squared with Norman's wife, still apparently alive for some years more in London, I never discovered, but it would seem that the arrangement was, by whatever subterfuge or careful non-statement of facts, quite amicable. I know this because I learnt that the wife's nephew and niece once enjoyed a happily remembered holiday visit there with their children. Through Zénaide's contacts, and despite his inadequate command of French, Norman became a well-established figure in the village and the surrounding countryside. He was often seen painting, in his cream flannel suit and his old straw hat with brushmarks on it. A number of his pictures of local scenes were given away as presents to friends and neighbours, and are prized objects in houses to this day.

Norman also got to work on the house, changing it in appearance from a very plain, slate-roofed, two-roomed French rural dwelling into something resembling an English *cottage orné* of the Edwardian period. He put up a trellis verandah along the front, painted the shutters and the gate blue, converted the grain-loft into two bedrooms reached by an inside, boxed-in ladder, and built on a kitchen and bathroom in a lean-to, with a soakaway to a covered pit beyond the apple trees. This was at a time when hardly another house in the vicinity had plumbing, for piped water only arrived in the village in 1965. Yet, within the two main rooms, he and Zénaide lived in the decor of past lives. I visited the place a number of times when he was there and it was still full of carved oak cupboards, embroidered chair seats and lace cloths. There was a photo of Zénaide, who was by then many years dead, displayed on a small table: a full-bodied, lively-looking woman in middle age, with dark curling hair. I wish I had paid more attention to it at the time, but I was not to know how significant the house and everyone connected with it were to become to me.

When Zénaide died of cancer in 1956 she left the house and all its contents to Norman *en usufruct*, that is to say, for his own lifetime but not to pass on to anyone else, a common arrangement under French law. Though she was gone and much missed, he gradually extended his stays over most of the year, for it seems that quite soon his wife in England was dead, too. By the time we got to know him he was getting old, and was inclined to tell long stories of which the point became obscured halfway through, but he was always very kind. One time when we invited him to dinner, he turned up with six large linen table-napkins as a present for us. Much later I realised that these napkins, each embroidered with an R and a D, must have formed part of the trousseau of Zénaide's ill-fated mother Blanche Daudon when she married the charming but feckless Charles Robin. We have those napkins still, well over a hundred years after they were stitched for a hopeful wedding that turned to grief.

When we returned to the village one spring, we found that the long, solitary winter had taken its toll on Norman. His memory seemed very poor and his speech was becoming incoherent, even in his own language. The village people were worried about him, too. He did not eat enough, said some, or wear warm enough clothes in cold weather, said another, while others were sure he had suffered some specific blow: a piece of bad news, perhaps – maybe a financial setback? Two kind women teachers from the local primary school became convinced he was suddenly impoverished, and each used some of her own modest savings to buy a picture from him.

In the summer he was no better, and when we reappeared the Mayor asked us if we could help find Norman's 'family in England' to come and rescue him? We knew that he had no family, as such, but recollected that he had liked to talk about his friendship with a well-known member of the British judiciary, his Honour Christmas Humphreys – famous incidentally, but in this case irrelevantly, for adopting the Buddhist faith long before it became fashionable. A judge was not hard to locate, even in those days well before the Internet, so we wrote the gentleman a careful letter and sent it off to the appropriate Inn of Court. Could he perhaps provide a name or address for any relatives of the late Mrs Lloyd?

It was some time before a reply came back to us, and meanwhile Norman had disappeared from the village without telling anyone where he was going. One early autumn day he had been seen getting onto the weekly bus into La Châtre, 'with his little suitcase and a roll of paintings'. Since then, there had been no news.

Three weeks later the Mayor received a call from a social worker in a Parisian public hospital. They had on one of their wards this old gentleman who had been found wandering and incoherent in the Métro. He had no belongings with him and no identifying papers, but patient conversation with him had eventually elucidated the name of the village, Chassignolles, as an address. After an abortive call to another village of the same name in the Massif Central, the social worker had eventually hit on the right one. How fortunate that even small places in France have retained a purely local administration, with someone in charge who knows everyone.

It was fortunate, too, that I happened to have returned to the village at that point for All Saints' Day, and so could undertake to seek Norman out in the hospital on my journey back to England. When I located him in a large public ward he was loquacious, and did not appear particularly unhappy, but was very confused. He claimed to have been attacked in the street, but the medical staff thought that he had had a stroke – *une attaque* indeed, in French, since that is apparently what a bad stroke can feel like to the sufferer.

When I got back to England my husband had at last just got a reply from the elderly judge. He had not, he said, seen his old acquaintance Lloyd for many years. He also revealed to us incidentally that the St John's Wood address had in fact been a boarding house kept by Mrs Lloyd, in which he himself had stayed, which rather confirmed our impression that Norman had innocently liked to talk up his social contacts. However, Christmas Humphreys also said that he thought Mrs Lloyd had had a nephew called Farrer, who had become a General Practitioner in Ribblesdale on the Lancashire–Yorkshire moors.

Since doctors can be located in registers just as judges can, at last contact was made with what turned out to be a kind and competent country doctor. By and by, with some interpretation help from us, Dr Farrer and his wife travelled to Paris, took charge of this long-unseen uncle-by-marriage (since there was no one else who could) and carried him back to an old people's home in the north of England. It seemed a bleak end to Norman's long and enterprising life, but it was a sensible solution and anyway the only one on offer. How the finances of care were settled, we did not like to ask; no doubt the doctor had substantial local influence.

Some months later, after lengthy to-ing and fro-ing between an English lawyer and a French one, each side uncomprehending of the other's language and legal system, it was agreed that, though the house now belonged to distant cousins of Zénaide, it was for the Farrers to deal with the contents. So Dr and Mrs Farrer travelled again to France and confronted a home that had been left untouched, with the bed damply made, clothes in the drawers and packets of food in the cupboards, for a whole winter, and in which mice, spiders, moths and the sheer passage of time had begun to do their worst. (We ourselves were at work far away in India at that point.) The Farrers spent several long days emptying the place, arranging the sale of what was saleable. They had to consign to a garden bonfire a mass of shredded and nibbled underwear, cushion covers and cloths. They also burnt a great many papers.

Among the papers, I heard some time afterwards, was a complete set of letters, all those Norman had written to Zénaide over the years of their liaison and all she had written to him, along with many, many photos. Mrs Farrer wrote to me: 'A real love story had gone on there, it was very touching, all their private world. But for that very reason it seemed right to burn the lot, so that's what we did.'

It occurred to me then to wonder if in fact the relationship between Norman and Zénaide dated from much earlier than the story of their meeting in Paris in 1944 would suggest. Did they move in the same circle between the wars, when Norman, from his London base, made trips to Paris? If so, on both sides the passionate romance was a clandestine one, kept secret by Norman from his wife in St John's Wood and by Zénaide from her series of Parisian gentlemen friends. A possible scenario,

which seemed more likely as I recalled how Norman had sometimes spoken to us of Zénaide 'when she was younger'. A scenario
now for ever irrecoverable.

How extremely lucky it was for me that the one thing the Farrers
did not burn was the little card-case with a crucifix on it. They
must have found it, with much else, in a crammed desk drawer,
parked it for the time being on the mantelpiece of the dead, cold
fireplace in the main room, and then just left it there because
they did not quite like to cast it onto the bonfire with everything
else. They cannot have looked inside it, as I did, when I eventually re-entered the house. They did not realise that what it contained was not religious cards but Célestine's hoarded proposals
of other marriages, alternative possible lives that she never lived,
all on the thin paper of the mid-nineteenth century, folded tight
and stuffed in.

So the reason I found the letters that, by and by, began to
gather so much importance for me was simply that the Farrers
were grateful to us. They knew we had done what we could for
Norman, and I had served as translator for the mutually uncomprehending lawyers. They wanted to offer us something from
the house as a keepsake. Remembering a footstool with a cat
embroidered on it in Berlin woolwork, I asked for that, and so
they left it in the otherwise emptied house for me to collect.
When I did so, later in the spring, there too was the inconspicuous card-case of letters that turned out to be such an
extraordinary treasure for me. It must be rare that such commonplace effort to help brings such a huge reward.

Norman died in the Lancashire care home several years
later. Dr John Farrer lived to ninety-two, we heard many years

afterwards, and died beloved by the whole area he had served. So I like to think that his habit of doing-what-he-could-to-help brought its reward, too.

Some fifteen years after Norman's death I received an overture from Australia, from a gallery in New South Wales.[18] The owners had some pictures by Norman Lloyd, knew of others and wanted to mount an exhibition of his work, but had been able to discover very little about his life. Then one of the owners had chanced upon my Célestine, Voice from a French Village in a bookshop and had realised that she had struck what, for a researcher, is gold. She contacted me through my publishers, and presently sent me copies of all the pictures they wanted to exhibit, hoping that I would be able to identify some of the locations around Chassignolles and La Châtre where the landscapes had been painted, which in many cases I could. I was also able to fill her in with information on Norman's happy life and its rather sad close.

So Norman's modest but enduring reputation in the art world has been restored. And in this saga of several lives, forgotten and then retrieved, I must add his own kindness and goodness into the equation. He made Zénaide's last dozen years really happy and, for that, villagers who remembered her as a girl, and knew of her family's sad decline, were grateful to him. In spite of his unorthodox behaviour, he evidently endeared himself enough to a little-seen nephew-by-marriage to make that man feel responsible towards him at the end. And had he not perseveringly befriended us with presents of wine, apples and napkins – and the insistent loan of a record player when he found me once in Chassignolles working on my own – I doubt whether we would have known enough about him to be able to set in train a rescue when he was in the Paris hospital, lost and alone. In that case, the cat-footstool would not have been waiting in the house for me and I would never have found the letters.

In Chassignolles today there is a rural museum, in a building we knew in the 1970s as a barn where the cows were milked. On the poster for the museum that greets visitors on the way into the village is proclaimed '*Village de Célestine*'. And in 2017, when an edict went out from the French government that, even in the countryside, roads must have official names and houses official numbers, the small road behind the church that runs past Célestine's one-time family cottage has been given her name.

CHAPTER VIII

Whole Worlds Were There

And some there be, which have no memorial; who are perished, as though they had never been; and are become as though they had never been born; and their children after them. But these were merciful men, whose righteousness hath not been forgotten ...

The Book of Ecclesiastes

Once into middle age, most of us come reluctantly to understand that our grandparents, often so three-dimensional and present to us, even fifty years after their deaths, are to younger generations just names on a family tree. At most, they are faces in old photographs or paintings, identifiable perhaps, but without memories attached. They are inexorably joining that host of the nameless 'merciful men', whose only discernible legacy is a generalised one. They are the people who lived their lives as best they could, procreated, 'came, and tilled the fields, and lay beneath', passed on some sense of decency and continuity to their descendants – and not always even that.

Virtually everyone I have ever interviewed about their family history, either in England or in France, has seemed happy to recount everything they knew, even discreditable facts, so fundamental is the desire that one's ancestors should not 'become as if they had never been born'. *Célestine, Voices from a French Village* was not published in French till several years after the British and American editions had appeared, and when the French translation was in preparation I made a round of all my most valued informants to ask them if they would prefer, for privacy's sake, for their forebears to appear in this edition under different names. To a man and woman they refused my offer, almost indignantly: they wanted their family stories identifiably preserved.

Some, I had already noticed, took particular pleasure from the way in which my research in censuses and other local records had corroborated and provided authentic dates for family events of which they had heard, but which they had been unable till then to situate accurately in time. For in folk and family memory there is a tendency for the generations to be compressed. Wanting to reach back and create a coherent story, or at any rate a manageable one, people will tend to refer to some colourful figure as a 'great-uncle', when cautious research reveals that he must have been a great-great-great one. They will claim a connection between, say, a minor Elizabethan landowner and a present-day farmer of the same name as if only two or three generations needed to be spanned. Or they will locate their family's arrival in the actual district only just beyond the reach of living memory ('My grandfather remembered that … ') when a careful perusal of documents suggests a far more distant link. In one part of my own family it was always claimed that sometime in the eighteenth century a single Tindall had travelled south from Scarborough (where the name is a common one) to the Kent–Sussex borders, where he and later his copious progeny settled. This turned out, upon research, to be substantially true – except that the sheer number of Tindall households already settled in several adjoining parishes, and sharing out the same small number of distinctive first names between them, were so plentiful already by the mid-eighteenth century that it seems clear the arrival of the original progenitor in the district must date from much earlier.

It is also possible that this ancestor, said to have come from a boat-building family, never existed in that particular identifiable way. He could have been the plausible suggestion of a helpful mentor: a Victorian clergyman, say. There were, indeed, boat-builders in Scarborough called Tindall in the eighteenth century: one I found buried in the cemetery overlooking the sea just behind the plot where Anne Brontë lies. But if it were once possible to trace a link between that dynasty and the one on the Kent–Sussex borders, the connection now seems irretrievable.

There is a considerable variation, even among people of more or less the same social level and kind, as to which families keep alive a sense of their joint history and which let it fade quickly into the void. One man who married into an established Chassignolles family found that his in-laws evoked distant relatives with pleasure and had a fund of ancient stories about them. He confided to me that he was sad when talk turned in that direction, because his own family had no such store: round their table the past had never been discussed. He evidently felt that his parents, and all the unknown generations lying behind them, had failed in some fundamental human duty of transmission – which I think they had. But there are many like them. One day, also in France, somewhere around the year 2010, a boy of about eighteen knocked shyly on our door. He revealed that he was the grandson of an old man who had been our neighbour in our first years in the village. This neighbour had died one Easter-time when late snow lay on the ground, and was laid out in state in his own bedroom for several days till the burial was arranged. That age-old custom was still, in the 1980s, just persisting. The boy told me that he knew little of his grandfather, a prominent local figure who was gone years before he himself had been born. His parents did not seem interested in describing the old man, and he wondered if perhaps, since I had mentioned him in my book, I could tell him a few more details? I did my best to oblige. It was evident that, by appearing, however fleetingly, on printed pages, the old man had acquired for his thoughtful young descendant an objective form and substance that casual family reference had not managed to impart.

An early-twentieth-century historian of rural France[19] wrote:

The written history of these regions is odd. It opens extremely late ... The country people who lived there, far from towns and main roads, remained for a long time without a voice of their own or anyone to speak for them. They were nevertheless there, they did things, cared about things, and thus had their effect, without anyone realising it, on the heart and soul of the nation. ('*But these were merciful men, whose righteousness hath not been forgotten ...*')

In rural France, till after the Revolution and the beginning of the nineteenth century, the parish records were kept in brief Latin by local priests, a bare recital of marriages, baptisms and burials. In any case, till well into the mid-century most ordinary country people were illiterate. The comparable country-dwellers of England were more fortunate, since England had had its Reformation two and a half centuries earlier. The Anglican Church encouraged its congregation to learn to read the Scriptures for themselves, and thus some degree of literacy became widespread. Not just registers but also accounts of parish affairs were written down, in English, and often quite loquaciously – a mine of incidental information for later generations.

Yet in England, too, there is great variation from one family to another as to which cherish links with their predecessors and which discard them, and this seems to have little to do with the perceived social status of these vanished people. My husband's family, for many generations, were employed in quite ordinary and unprestigious ways in the wool business of the West Country, around Bath and Trowbridge. According to records, they were fleece-treaters, wool-dyers and woollen cloth-dressers, earlier they had probably been shepherds. One day in the mid-nineteenth century an enterprising son took the newly established railway line to London and set up a small greengrocer's shop in Hampstead. The business must have prospered, for his own son grew up to found a livery stable, which was an economic and social step up from both wool-dying and cabbage-selling, and the next generation continued the business, eventually switching from horse-hire to car-hire. Yet though, like so many others at the time, they had exchanged a timeless, pre-industrial world of

essentially rural labour for the very different tempo of expanding Victorian and Edwardian London, it is evident from successive censuses that their ties to Trowbridge remained unbroken.
Small children were sent there for holidays, and the livery-
stable founder retired back there in old age and raised chickens
in sufficient numbers to style himself, in the Census of 1911, 'egg
and poultry dealer'. Eggs were apparently sent up to town, to the
stables, and sold there during the First World War as a welcome
addition to London's haphazard rationing system.

The Lansdowns (for such was their indisputably West
Country name, that of a hill just outside Bath) evidently took
a pride in their rural origins, sufficient to make some member
of the family, in the 1930s, commission a family tree. It is clear
that the genealogist who undertook the job knew his business –
which is to say that he knew that, when presented with an
English family who had stayed in much the same part of the
country for centuries, there would be a connection, however
remote, with all the other families whose history was similarly
static. The simple geometric progression by which individual
ancestors accumulate as the generations go back (two grandparents, four great-grandparents, eight great-great-grandparents,
and so on till the supposed numbers form a multitude vastly
greater than any whole population) ensures that in practice the
same individuals are replicated many times over. Sure enough,
some distant link was found between the Lansdowns and a
modestly landed family (the Scudamores), and hence, by what
was clearly a series of authenticated and well-practised leaps,
with the nobility of medieval England, thus inevitably with its
kings, then with European royalty and finally – hooray! – with
the Emperor Charlemagne. Satisfaction all round.

(Had the family origins indicated an Eastern input, the ultimate triumphantly-named ancestor would have been Genghis Khan.)

Yet how different was the relationship with the past shown by a member of what, on the face of it, would appear to have been a similar family of origin. This man, about 1930, became the father-in-law of a Lansdown son. His family name was Camp, and like the Lansdowns in Wiltshire – or indeed the Tindalls in Sussex, and innumerable other people all over the British Isles – the Camps in Essex seem to have been employed for generations at work on the land. I say 'seem' because the fact was never mentioned. Harry Camp was a police constable in Hampstead, a well-known local figure. He and his wife had managed to get a transfer to that salubrious spot when she complained successfully (probably with dramatic demonstrations) that the bad air of his original posting, to Woolwich, was affecting her lungs. It was an astute move. In Hampstead the couple's two children grew up in a policeman's tied cottage with a garden, and the neighbours and the regular fellow-attenders at the local Baptist chapel were distinctly more genteel than the dockers of Woolwich or, indeed, the labourers of Essex.

If Harry ever ruminated on his childhood in a probably cramped and comfortless Essex dwelling, he did not mention it. Neither his daughter nor his grandson, both of whom lived with him till his death in the early 1950s, had any idea how many brothers and sisters he had had: he never seemed to want to speak of them or to talk of what they might have become, let alone get in touch with them. He always claimed, probably correctly, to have had only two years at school, which then cost two old pennies a week. It was known that as a young man he had worked 'on the roads', laying tarmac and paving for districts of new houses as late-nineteenth-century London inexorably expanded. This was no doubt better paid than work in the fields. He was tall and well-built and it was suggested to him that the Metropolitan Police might be interested in having a recruit such as him. He applied, but was told that he would have to improve his writing skills: evidently the two years at school, just enough to acquire the ability to read and do simple arithmetic, had not extended to handwriting and spelling adequate for a constable. So he went to evening classes to improve, reapplied and was accepted. Thus set on the road to a different social milieu, he seems to have left his origins firmly behind him.

His wife did not share his reticence. She herself came from an East End family called Montague, who were colourful and barely respectable. Her father was said (truthfully or otherwise) to have been a fishmonger who went bankrupt because he drank too much. Her maternal grandfather, Solomon Joel, had been a pedlar of sponges, which suggests an origin in a Jewish immigration to Britain long pre-dating the usual East End arrival in the late-Victorian period. She was the oldest of fourteen children, and claimed that she never went to school because she was needed at home to mind the younger ones and anyway preferred it that way. She had several relatives with eccentric habits, who were nevertheless welcomed in the tidy Hampstead police cottage, where their doings provided an interesting background saga. A little Montague niece was even taken in as a foster-child when her parents were in difficulties. Apparently it was his *own* relations Harry Camp wished to cut out of his life, not anyone else's.

Were any of the Camps killed in the First World War? There seemed no information, and the surname is sufficiently common that it is difficult now to research. A search through national death-records did turn up, in recent years, what appeared to be a brother of Harry's who was run over at night by a cart near Chadwell Heath, but such a tragedy had never been mentioned. Was there, one wonders, something in the Camp family, some brush with the law, that made them – if you were a respectable police constable – relations to be avoided? Had Harry walked out of the family home in one of his tempers and never gone back? Or was it simply that, still in the early twentieth century as in all the centuries before, if you moved away from your home territory and there was little family ability at writing and no question of a telephone, contact was all too easily lost?

Only when he was well on in life, had retired from the police and was working as a porter at a specialised Hampstead hospital did Harry pick up a family thread. A young man on one of the wards had a rather unusual surname, which Harry recognised as the same as that of a man who, long ago, had been courting a Camp sister. It turned out that the young man was Harry's nephew. He was polite and pleasant, and with him at least some contact was at last established.

Of the furnishings and knick-knacks that Harry and Esther Camp acquired over the years, with goodness knows how much labour and saving, carried with them from Woolwich to Hampstead and finally bequeathed to their daughter, almost nothing remains – as you would expect. The cycle from prized object to discarded one to rubbish, and then to extinction, is a well-established one: it is only the occasional object that survives to remount the scale of value, becoming again, if not useful, at any rate 'quaint' and then, just possibly, objectively valuable. Almost every edition of the long-running televised *Antiques Roadshow* produces some vase abandoned in an attic or memento brought back by a soldier from the far side of the world that turns out to be worth a modest, or very occasionally huge, sum of money.

Nothing that Harry and Esther Camp possessed was ever likely to fall into the latter category, but among a very few surviving objects of theirs – antiquated garden implements, a last for mending shoes upon, a hand-made wooden box – is a decorative plate with worn gilt flowers around its edges. The centre figures a lover-and-his-lass, in the garments of the early nineteenth century, she with a basket of flowers that she might be offering for sale, he in an improbably striped tailcoat and a shovel-shaped working hat, which looks oddly un-English. Indeed a small *schloss*-like building appears in the background, above a classic balustrade, and on the back of the plate is printed 'Bavaria' and a simple coat-of-arms. Bavaria was a centre for eighteenth- and nineteenth-century porcelain-making.

This plate can never have been an expensive one, since its picture is printed rather than hand-painted, but it was, for whatever reason, valued by the Camp couple, and this sense of its value was passed on to their daughter and thence to their grandson. Which is why, when both Harry and Esther have been dead for well over fifty years, the plate stands today on our kitchen dresser in a house in Kentish Town, north London, beside Italian and French ones. It is the kind of mass-produced memento that was bought as a 'fairing', a present from a fair that a young man would offer his girl, an alternative to bonny-blue ribbons. Indeed, there seems to be a just-surviving whisper about someone having bought it for someone else, in some dateless past time.

I don't think Harry Camp bought it for Esther. That would not have been his style, and anyway it seems to belong earlier than their late-Victorian youth, to a world where shops with such articles were few outside the towns, and much of what is now townscape was still open countryside with heaths, flocks of sheep and cattle, pedlars – and fairs. Did a long-forgotten Camp buy it in Essex for his future wife, who treasured it because she never had much else from him later but curses and babies? Did Solomon Joel give it to his bride Ann Beavis, in the days when Whitechapel was the end of London and Mile End Road still stretched between fields, fine gardens, endowed almshouses and the oldest Jewish cemetery in England? Irrecoverable. But the plate has survived.

Traditionally, the populations of British cities have long been considered further removed from their rural origins than their French counterparts, mainly because the industrial revolution arrived much later in France and more partially, leaving great tracts of that large, fertile country hardly touched by industry. Still today, grandparents or great-uncles and -aunts rooted in a French countryside where their forebears have lived for generations are a part of life for many families in Paris, Lille or Lyons, and there is much spending of holidays with country cousins. In Britain the links tend to be too distant in time for contact to have been maintained: the shepherds and milkmaids who left the land in droves to go into the mines and mills are remote, unknowable. Yet even in the late-Victorian London,

Manchester or Birmingham of street markets, of corner pubs and cramped housing, of back yards and innumerable smoking chimneys, some sense of the countryside's presence not far off still lingered. Well into the twentieth century horses still clopped around city streets, bringing smells of country dust and straw and stables and a half-memory of country ways in among the engine-fumes and the clang of trams. The names of many of the town pubs themselves – the Ploughman's Rest, the Bull and Last, the Woodman's Arms – bore testimony to the country setting in which they had so recently stood, and do so even today. Cramped town back-gardens still continue to support isolated mature trees that, a hundred or more years ago, were survivors of orchards or hedgerow lines that had recently occupied that land. Till about the 1860s and the accelerating proliferation of railway suburbs, it was not difficult to walk out of any big urban centre, even London. Hackney Wick was still fields, as was Earls Court and much of North Kensington. Hampstead Heath, the Londoners' traditional playground, was not the green oasis in a great urban mass that it was later to become, but was separated from Camden Town and Swiss Cottage by open country, and adjoined further fields running towards the isolated crossroads that was Golders Green.

So lovers and lasses still took country walks on fine days, stopping by at real country pubs with sawdust on the floor. And even in the music halls, those centres of working-class town enjoyment, full of risqué jokes about the big bad world out there in the streets all around, a perception of country pleasures was present in the songs. The boy loved by the girl onstage might be 'up in the gallery', surrounded by rococo plasterwork and gazing down at her through the theatre lights, but he was still perceived, in Marie Lloyd's famous song, as being 'as merry as a robin that sings on a tree'.

Even today, when many town and suburban children reputedly don't even know that milk comes from cows, our language is resonant with metaphors from a lost world of both nature and obsolete skills. Enterprises *bear fruit*, we don't *let the grass grow under our feet*, we get things *cut and dried*, we *make hay while the sun shines*, we *save up for a rainy day*, we *break the ice*, we discourage others from *going on a wild-goose chase*. Information is *grist to our mill*, we *upset the apple cart*, have various *irons in the fire* or *strike while the iron is hot*, condemn some course of action as *putting the cart before the horse* or *shutting the stable door when the horse has bolted* or *kicked over the traces*. We *get the bit between our teeth* – even though relatively few people today have the knowledge as to exactly how doing that results in action uncontrolled by anyone else, or even what a 'bit' is.

Lansdown, Camp, Tindall: I have used these families as exemplars that come to hand because that is what they are: they represent a multitude of similar people, who have no memorial, but have gone collectively to shape the world we still live in today. So, too, with their own rather more exotic contribution, have the Montagues and the Joels: they stand for the huge, continuing saga of emigration from distant lands that has also formed us. I could offer further names from my own side of the family: that of even earlier immigrants, Huguenot ancestors who brought their metal-working skills to England at the end of the seventeenth century; also the dynasty of Anglo-Irish country surgeons who will indeed put in an appearance shortly. Rather better-documented, these lots, but nonetheless all gone, with their passions, their energies, their achievements and their failures, and almost, if not quite, forgotten.

My grandsons bear the name that their solid, blue-eyed ancestors bore on Lansdown Hill near Bath, when for generations they tended sheep and cleaned and carded the wool and spun and dyed it. But these young Lansdowns have the dark eyes of another strain in the woven tissue of their genes. Their forefathers for more than a hundred years ran a ferry across the Arno, just upriver of Florence. These men too had practical phrases, in their case to do with water and currents, wind and weather. Some of these remain in present-day Italian, transformed into metaphors that suggest whole stories. *Avere acqua alla gola* – literally, to be in water up to your throat – is to be involved in any situation too deeply. The similar foreboding that *L'acquae chete rovinano i ponte* – waters that seem calm may still overwhelm the bridge – can shift back from a figurative to a literal one even today. What is hoped for is that *l'affare e andato in porto*: the deal has finally been done – that is, it has ended up well. The boat has docked, a safe haven has been reached from time's rolling stream.

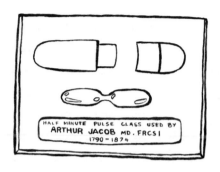

HALF MINUTE PULSE GLASS USED BY
ARTHUR JACOB MD. FRCSI
1790-1874

CHAPTER IX

The Pulse Glass. And Other Measures of Emotion

The early-twentieth-century historian G.M. Trevelyan[20] famously wrote: 'Once, on this earth, once on this familiar spot of ground, walked other men and women, as actual as we are today, thinking their own thoughts, swayed by their own passions, but now all gone, one generation vanishing after another, gone as utterly as we ourselves shall shortly be gone like ghosts at cockcrow.'

I have tended to assume, this far, that the complete disappearance of the ghosts in most families, once several generations have passed, must be a matter of regret, and that the survival of such solidly documented ghosts as Margaret Paston, the first Venetia Stanley or the successive Ralph, Edmund and John Verneys is a matter of public congratulation and also of good fortune. Very few ordinary families have, of course, the space, the leisure or the tradition of houses handed on from one generation to another to achieve this level of memory preservation, even if they want to. Moves, changes of circumstances, marriages into different milieux – these things tend to work against keeping the family records. Or do they? Sometimes displacement, and the collapse of a way of life, seems to lead to more fervent conservation and the creation of a new archive, as a defence against further loss.

My father's mother, Blanche Jacob, born in 1875, grew up in a classic Anglo-Irish Dublin household a generation before that world disintegrated. She was one of the younger daughters among the ten children of a Dublin doctor, with a particular speciality in diseases of the eye. The Jacob family (the name seems to be Quaker rather than Jewish) had acquired lands in Ireland under Oliver Cromwell, founded a dynasty of country surgeons in Maryborough and Sligo, and by the nineteenth century was ensconced in the Protestant Ascendancy. Although medical men did not, strictly speaking, count as landed gentry, the Jacob family were well known, and the fact that the Dublin Dr Jacob was a physician accredited to Dublin Castle, where the Viceroy presided over a miniature Ruritanian court, meant that the Jacob ladies were invited to Castle receptions and were 'presented' there at the age of eighteen. Dr Jacob, as well as fathering so many children, was no businessman, so the family never had quite enough money to sustain the big house in Ely Place and the lifestyle that was expected of them. However, they managed, from one grocer's bill crisis to another and, judging from the various accounts they wrote later in life, were most of the time happy.

The previous medical occupant of the Ely Place house, and the first one in Dublin to take an interest in diseases of the eye, had been Blanche's grandfather, Dr Arthur Jacob, from whom her father had inherited the practice. Arthur Jacob (born in 1795) was a distinguished, eccentric and eventually rather difficult man, who had been the first in the Jacob dynasty to take a proper medical degree and had, as a young man, walked perseveringly from Edinburgh all the way to the south coast of England and then on to Paris to complete his studies. Blanche never knew this gentleman personally, since he died, aged eighty, a few months before she was born, and anyway had taken himself off some years before to live with a son in England. Yet it was with Blanche that his pulse glass ended up, which is why it is in my house to this day.

It is a little ivory case not much longer or fatter than a stick of chalk. It unscrews, and within is a tiny elongated hourglass half-filled with fine, reddish sand. Only it is not, of course, an hourglass, but an exact half-minute glass, designed for taking a patient's pulse. Doctors have 'felt' pulses from Hippocratic and especially from Galenic times almost to the present day. Pulse glasses date from the era when an ordinary pocket-watch did not have a second-hand to enable the doctor to time the number of heartbeats in thirty seconds. Watches with this refinement did begin to come in during the seventeenth century, and by the end of the eighteenth were part of the equipment of the fashionable practitioner, but were still beyond the reach of the ordinary young doctor. Arthur Jacob seems to have acquired his traditional pulse glass during his stay in Paris, where such elegant little accessories were made, and used it in the early years of the practice that he set up in Dublin. It was probably outdated by the time he was in middle life, for the classic image of the Victorian doctor is of a frock-coated practitioner, watch in one hand, early version of a stethoscope in the other. But evidently Arthur was attached to it, kept it, and after his death it was enshrined in a small case, suitably labelled, by his son.

But this does not quite explain why, when her family was split up and scattered far and wide, it was Blanche, rather than her doctor elder brother, who got the pulse glass.

The whole self-confident world of the Anglo-Irish was, by the time Blanche was growing up, destined to end. Long after, when she had spent most of her adult life in England, and had acquired a degree of perception that her staunchly Unionist family had always lacked, she wrote in a memoir for her children: 'Looking back dispassionately on the people among whom my youth was spent, I can see that even in their hey-day they were doomed to extinction … Their end came violently, and they left Ireland with their houses burning behind them, but though it might have come more gradually and more kindly … It would have come inevitably.' By the time she wrote that, she had lost most of her Dublin intonation, except when telling a joke, and regarded herself, with an ironic humour that had become her hallmark, as 'a fairly satisfactory example of the conventional British matron'. She had lived very comfortably for decades in still-just-about rural Hertfordshire.

How did this come about? When Blanche was in her early twenties, and one of only three sisters and one brother still at home, her father died suddenly, leaving his widow and these remaining children in abrupt and unforeseen poverty. No more big house, no more holidays by the sea or parties at the Castle. The boy, at just seventeen, was shipped off summarily to Canada to seek his fortune. Neither of the other two young sisters ever married, but eked out submerged lives as, respectively, a residential nurse and a school matron, in London's displaced Anglo-Irish community. Blanche would no doubt have had to do the same – except that a business associate of her late father was a Tindall of obscure rural origins who had, in the entre-preneurial hothouse of late-Victorian London, become a successful medical publisher. With an eye, no doubt, to strength-ening his firm's connection with the Dublin medical world, and to acquiring sole rights in the professional journal that he and Dr Jacob had published together, he suggested to the widowed Mrs Jacob that Blanche come and spend a holiday in his big house in Kent. His younger daughter, he wrote, would be a nice companion for her, and his elder son, Bertie, had seen a photo-graph of Blanche and was 'quite smitten' by her.

Blanche must have known what was expected of her, and that this was probably her one big chance. Bertie, too, who was shy and rather under his father's powerful thumb, also knew what he was supposed to do. I have written about Bertie and Blanche elsewhere[21] and when I did so, I imagined, as had other relatives, that each of them had sensibly made the best of a marriage neither of them had exactly chosen. But I was wrong – for a cache of letters, which only came to my knowledge after my book was published, and decades after Bertie and Blanche were both dead, proved otherwise.

Bertie was a hoarder. His mother had died when he was thirteen, and from then on he developed a lifetime habit of making scrapbooks of newspaper cuttings and photographs. Once he had left school he also kept a record, year on year, in identical little Letts diaries, of his daily doings. For the lonely boy, striving to behave properly and to satisfy his father by going into the family firm (not something he had chosen to do, either), the limited spaces of the diaries became a repository of his most private thoughts, both hopeful and agonised. But later, as he settled down into his life's duties, he evidently did not need the diary-outlet so much, for it became instead a simple record of his financial outgoings, day on day and year on year. Thus an ordinary weekday might read: 'Lunch 11d. Papers 8d. Omnibus 1d. Tobacco 1s.2d.'; while on high days and holidays, such as one during his honeymoon with Blanche in Ireland, there is noted: 'Cycles booked 2s. Porter 6d. Tickets £1.19s.2d. Tea baskets 2s.' The Sunday when his first child was born includes 'Stamps and telegrams, 3s.1d.' and the following day a sum for an 'advertisement in the *Morning Post*, 5s.' Over many years, a complete life is revealed, but only in outline and by inference.

How do I know all this? Because he stored up the diaries his whole life, through several house-moves, and kept much else besides, including literally hundreds of letters. When he died, at well over ninety (Blanche had been dead for fifteen years), there was a brief post-funeral visit to his attic to assess the contents. This mass of material was visibly stacked, quite neatly, in boxes. I remarked that all this stuff might be of some archival value, but older relatives were made uneasy, resistant to the idea that I, or anyone, might have a legitimate interest here. What to me was long-past history to be retrieved and perhaps preserved was, to them, still potent and too close for comfort. But something was evidently at work within me: it was one of those moments, as in the deserted cottage in France, when the future opens up before you, without you realising it. While no one was looking, I grabbed a handful of the diaries and stashed them away in my handbag.

Many years passed. Writing a book[22] about a network of family connections in Paris over two hundred years, I retrieved the diaries from the back of my own now-substantial archive cupboard. I made use of the daily entries Bertie had written in

Paris as a struggling eighteen-year-old, sent there to learn French and the book trade. By this time aunts were all dead, my own father was very old. He now seemed quite pleased to hear that I had rescued the diaries and was researching into more distant family history. He gave me Arthur Jacob's pulse glass to keep. He died (in his nineties, like his father and grandfather) before I had quite finished the book. I was therefore able to complete it with some rather more frank passages than I would have felt able to include if he had still been living.

I had supposed that all the rest of the massed papers I had seen in Bertie's attic forty years before had long since become flame and dust. Only after my father was dead, and the book was already in the process of being printed, did I get a telephone call alerting me to 'a big box of papers in the barn that looks like letters belonging to your side of the family'. The call was from the son of my father's third wife. Twice a widower, my father had instantly married again, in his seventies, and had gone to live in this third wife's large and rather remote house, taking few personal possessions with him. How it had come about that this collection of papers had survived the normal processes of destruction and had actually followed him from one home to another, when so much else was discarded, I cannot fathom, but my barely known step-relative was right. The huge, collapsing box was duly collected from the barn by my brother and his wife, and at once brought by them to me in London. Mementoes of long-past family were not my brother's thing. There were all the letters, cards, further diaries, notes and newspaper cuttings that I had glanced at hastily in an attic a lifetime ago. When I could, I settled down to the substantial task of reading my way through them.

*

It soon became apparent that Bertie was not alone in his hoard-
ing. Blanche had been as much of a letter-keeper as he was;
and it was from material she must have kept that I discovered
that, however heavily contrived their initial meeting had been,
some chemistry had soon got to work, transforming a wordly
arrangement into something other. Bertie's first letter to her,
when Blanche's visit to the Tindalls was being set up in the
summer of 1905, was written with sober formality – 'Dear Miss
Jacob, I shall be most happy to meet you at Euston' – but by the
later autumn a quite different note was being struck:

> Darling Blanche. I am so happy to think that I shall see you
> again on Friday evening. I have arranged about the bicycles
> and sent a message to book the private dining parlour in our
> favourite inn …

A little later in the winter, when their engagement had been
announced (multiple letters of congratulation to Bertie were
also in the box) came a still more lyrical and explicit note:

> The sofa we chose together has arrived, so soon we shall have
> a chance to be in our favourite position! We must try not to be
> too violent, my darling, but I don't feel that, even once the
> honeymoon is over, our feelings are going to change, do you?

Goodness. I don't imagine this particular letter meant exactly
what it would mean today, but all the same …

I should record that their feelings apparently did not change,
since during the almost-fifty years of married life they had
together, every time Bertie was away on a business trip or Blanche

had gone to stay with one sister or another, they wrote each other turn by turn every single day. All these letters seem to have been kept by each of them.

They were not, in fact, ideally suited to one another. Blanche was far more outgoing than Bertie, loving to fill the house, Dublin-style, with relatives and friends. She was a good raconteur and, like many people with more intelligence than education, could be manipulative and demanding. She was also bossy. Bertie, as the son of an overbearing father, and with a similarly forceful elder sister, had developed his own tacit resistance to such things. He liked a quieter life, had a way of absenting himself, mentally, if not physically, did not ordinarily go in for enthusiasm, and on rare occasions could lose his temper spectacularly. The quiet passion of his life was art, and especially architecture. On holiday, Baedeker in hand, he loved to tour the galleries and cathedrals and castles of Europe, and could keep at it all day. Blanche did not care deeply for such things but, being a good wife, she bravely accompanied him ('Oh Bertie dear … My *feet* … ').

The strong bond that held them together was, I think, that each had suffered an irreparable loss in youth. Bertie had lost his loving, quiet, rather intellectual mother to a sudden illness when he was on the brink of adolescence, and was left to the mercy of his loud, domineering father. Blanche had lost, at her own father's death, the whole world of cheerful, hospitable Anglo-Irish life, as well as the prestige of belonging to a renowned family of doctors. Each did their very best, in marriage, to re-create variously the love, the companionship, the status, the protective environment and the fun that they separately so missed.

It helped, of course, that they were comfortably off. On marriage, rising thirty, Bertie was made a partner in the medical publishing firm, which was doing very well, thanks to the relent-less work-ethic and entrepreneurial flair of Albert Alfred senior. For Blanche, life in Hertfordshire, within easy reach of London, brought her the secure, comfortable, even lavish lifestyle to which the Dublin Jacobs had aspired, but had never quite achieved. She turned their home into a chief gathering place for her own scattered relations and for Bertie's, and when the Great War came, their house became the refuge in which brothers, brothers-in-law and nephews found a ready welcome on their leaves from the front – from which, classically, three never returned. Their stiff-upper-lip letters, and still more poignant last notes, pencil-written from the trenches where they met their deaths, are of course among the collection.

Even before Bertie came into her life, Blanche must have been squirrelling away mementoes – including, evidently, Arthur Jacob's pulse glass. How many long-gone heartbeats had it measured? Among the other old items are several envelopes containing minute curls in tissue paper, the hair of babies newborn to elder sisters and brothers when Blanche herself was a young girl, some hundred and twenty years ago. Should they ever have been kept beyond a year or two? Probably not. But now that they have been … There is an entire packet, tied with ribbon, of letters she received when her own children were born ('I'm sure Bertie must be pleased. Men always want a little girl, I'm told!'). The habit of keeping everything grew on her and Bertie, if anything, with the years. There are many missives of the 1920s and '30s from an Arthur who was some kind of step-cousin to Bertie – the dynamic Albert Alfred senior had, of course, replaced Bertie's dead mother with a second wife, who brought with her a string of slightly eccentric relations. Arthur, like a cartoon character, seems to have been perpetually 'on his uppers', selling second-hand cars on commission and grovellingly grateful for Blanche and Bertie's hospitality and 'help', which one must suppose was money.

And there are other anguished letters of the 1930s from the baby daughter, now transformed into a determined Oxford grad-uate whose choice of fiancé did not meet with her parents' standards of acceptability. Evidently the experience of genteel poverty, counting as social and personal failure, that had haunted Blanche during her protracted girlhood till marriage rescued her, had gone deep. She had apparently set her heart on her daughter marrying 'well', regardless that the daughter had turned into a rather bookish and principled person who was unlikely to make a worldly match.

The young man that daughter Monica had met at Oxford had been educated at an acceptable Scottish public school, but once he had finished university he was without resources and emerged into adult life in the depths of the 1929–30 economic recession. He was also, not surprisingly in these circumstances, a Socialist. Bertie and Blanche kept shipping Monica off for protracted visits to other countries, hoping that in new surround-ings she would 'get over' Brian, but to no avail. One sealed envelope turned out to preserve a clean copy of what Bertie himself wrote to her at the height of this years-long drama: 'Do not imagine that your mother and I will ever cease to love you or will cut you off with a shilling, but you must realise that we cannot approve of Brian and never will …'

But approval was the one thing their daughter, loving and dutiful by nature, wanted. At last, after eight years of rows and misery, the marriage took place, in secret, at the outbreak of war in 1939. It lasted happily for more than fifty years, and of course after the war Monica's parents became quite reconciled to Brian, now respectably employed as a schoolmaster. So why was all the painful correspondence not thrown away? A darker, more obsessional aspect to Bertie and Blanche's habit of preservation becomes apparent.

If this mass of material were letters relating to my own life, my own contemporaries, I would almost certainly destroy it. If you dredge forgotten letters, out of a long-undisturbed file or box, does what you find still constitute part of your identity? Or does the fact that you have forgotten about them for so long mean they have become irrelevant to your present self and should be thrown away? (As a philosophy or psychology exam might say: Discuss.)

But Bertie and Blanche, and most of the people they ever knew, have now vanished from living memory, so the argument runs differently. Undying love, daily trivia, tragedy, passion, gratitude, resentment, extinct quarrels, the process of the garden in forgotten summers ... Forty years ago all this might have been regarded as expendable, just Over. But now that it has survived so long, and so much against the odds – why did my father, a mover-on in life, never throw it all out himself? – it has accrued an extra freight of meaning. And that historical freight deepens subtly with each passing year.

Did someone, sometime in the rising modernity of the sixteenth century, seriously consider getting rid of all those encumbering letters from dead-and-gone Paston relations who could not even write fair English? Very likely. But they didn't do it.

Much as I should like, in a way, to be rid of all this paper, I am not quite sure that it has yet reached the end of its long, precarious, but tenacious existence.

CHAPTER X

The Past Destroyed

It may be felt that the destruction and the losses sustained by Bertie Tindall and Blanche Jacob were not of an especially terrible kind. But Bertie's mother had died suddenly, from typhoid, a disease carried by unclean food or water, which was not by then a common fate in a comfortably-off middle-class household. She had gone to Kent to retrieve a sick daughter who had been sent for a supposedly healthy holiday to Tindall in-laws on a farm. The daughter recovered, but the mother fell ill. This absurd and tragic outcome effectively seems to have put an end to relations between the successful Albert Alfred in London and the rest of the modestly rural Tindall clan. Bertie grew up knowing none of them; another loss, though unspoken. As for Blanche's close relatives, they had left Ireland for careers elsewhere by the time the Troubles that led to Independence began in earnest. Unlike many of their kind, they did not see their own houses burnt. But they lost their world all the same, and not all of them thrived.

*

In comparison, the more distant losses and dramas suffered by both the Paston and the Verney families were far more dramatic. Death came readily, and often unpredictably, in earlier centuries, even when it was not helped along by civil wars and brutal retaliations, which it often was. Fine houses were attacked and sometimes destroyed, and gentlemen were imprisoned or executed. All these events were enumerated in letters; along with cheerful descriptions of social events, energetic match-making, and irritation with wayward sons or brothers.

Worse things happened on the Continent. In central France, during the Hundred Years War of the fourteenth and fifteenth centuries, the mercenaries employed by the English did not hesitate to destroy crops and cattle, set farmhouses and barns alight, kill indiscriminately. For centuries, throughout Europe, ill-paid soldiers with no personal allegiances were allowed to sack the towns they conquered and carry off booty, killing and raping as they went. In theory, by the twentieth century, such behaviour was relegated to the barbaric past. There was even by then a fairly widespread belief that war between 'civilised' nations, who were also trading partners, was now impossible. Various international conventions were signed to this effect, and also aimed to outlaw the worst forms of modern assault, such as toxic gases. However, this did not stop the supposedly principled German *Junkers* under Kaiser Wilhelm from invading neutral Belgium in 1914, shooting large numbers of the inhabitants for daring to resist, sacking Louvain and burning down its medieval library, complete with a huge number of irreplaceable books and manuscripts. Gas attacks followed not long after.

The horror of such assaults hardly needs labouring, and nor does the fact that such things have happened in still more recent times and are with us today – indeed, are present more than ever since the re-entry of Faith into politics over a significant part of the world. In countries where some concept of the 'rules of war' is in operation, however sketchily, the murder of hapless civilians is not usually a direct intention, but such is the indiscriminate power of modern weaponry that it inevitably takes place. Urban areas are battered, made uninhabitable and ultimately flattened unrecognisably. Homes, businesses and the whole context of people's lives are destroyed. Sometimes, however, it seems that this is a primary intention of the assailants, whether by sophisticated long-range attacks from the air or by home-made devices set off by individuals in crowded streets, as inflicted in our time on the unfortunate citizens of Iraq, Afghanistan and Syria. In the same way, the obliteration of habitat and especially townscape that took place in the Second World War across Britain, Germany and elsewhere incidentally caused many deaths, but was essentially intended to destroy those societies' structures and turn the recent past into a lost country. As Milan Kundera has famously said, though in the context of totalitarianism rather than overt destruction: 'The first step in liquidating a people is to erase its memory. Destroy its books, its culture, its history.'[23] Such, too, is the message of George Orwell's 1984.

It is hardly surprising, and a sign of human courage and persistence, that after such destructive wars citizens returning to a devastated place will often demand that it be rebuilt as it was before, a rebuilding of memory. After the Second World War the capital of Poland, deliberately wrecked by the Nazi forces, was laboriously reconstructed, not as a new, concrete twentieth-century metropolis, but in appearance as it had been,

including the Old City. More recently, renowned buildings in
Dresden that had disappeared in RAF fire-bombing have been
re-erected also. In Bosnia, the famous Mostar Bridge, built in
the sixteenth century by Ottoman Turks over the River Nereta
and completely obliterated by Croatians in the civil war in 1993,
today triumphantly spans the river again, looking as if it had
never been gone. The Bosnians do not regard this as the
'Disneyfication' of their past, at which some Western observers
hint, but as the reclaiming of their own history.

Similarly, in the First World War, when whole small villages
in Flanders were wiped off the map, never to return, the medieval city of Ypres was left so comprehensively ruined that it was
seriously suggested it should be left that way permanently, by
way of a memorial. The suggestion was indignantly turned down
by the returning citizens, and today a carefully rebuilt Ypres is
a far better memorial to the abiding nature of loss than any ruin
could be. The restored Menin Gate is the location, every single
evening, of a Last Post ceremony, at which there are always
attenders from both far and near. The idea – current circa 1970 –
that this ritual must gradually die away has proved to be entirely
mistaken. The millions of men whose names are inscribed on
that Gate and other memorials throughout the area have now
passed, as individuals, from human memory, but their collective
significance has grown rather than diminished with time.

(Obviously, in the very long run, this memory too will be
extinguished, along with all else. We do not mourn the dead of
Bronze Age tribal battles, and even the named victims of the
Battle of Hastings are too far in time from us for any sense of
identification. This, too, is a further example of the long, long
metamorphosis of time.)

*

The devastating loss of home, culture, belongings and often of loved family members too, as suffered by refugees in our own time, has all happened before, many times, and to huge numbers of people. It is a fact of human nature that we can empathise more readily with a specific person than with a multitude, but in doing so we are accurately perceiving the true nature of such loss by relating one sufferer's ultimate fate to their original and personal identity. The thought of the millions killed in the Nazi concentration camps horrifies us intellectually, but we identify with the iconic figure of the teenage Anna Frank who has, by the random chance of her diary surviving, come to stand for all of them. She is not 'one of those six million': she is someone like ourselves, a teenager chafing within a restricted life, falling in love with a boy because he is there and her swelling emotional capacity needs an outlet. Similarly when the clothed, intact body of a boy of three was washed up in 2015 on a Turkish beach, when the refugee boat taking him and his Syrian family to Greece foundered, this captured the world's imagination more than all the other images of overladen dinghies. Many, many other very young children have drowned, often along with their parents, in similar circumstances, but this is the one singled out for remembrance. Uninjured, just dead, in his shorts and T-shirt, he looked like the three-year-old belonging to any one of us, when asleep.

The same narrow but valid sense of personal recognition is evident in a letter written by the young Maria Josepha Holroyd,[24] who later would marry the first Lord Stanley. (She was to become, sixty years later, the old lady who hopefully foresaw the invention of the telephone, and lived on into her nineties as a representative of the world that had gone.) Writing in 1793, when the French Revolution across the Channel was reaching its murderous climax, she mentioned the destitute and shoeless situation of four French refugees she had encountered in Guy's Hospital, London, where her family had some kind of influence. These were, she wrote, 'gentlemen and officers … grateful to be accepted by a common hospital', who had escaped from imprisonment on a French ship by swimming to an English shore, and then barely scraped enough coins together to get a ride to London: 'It really makes one's blood run cold to think what extremities hundreds are reduced to, and what a number of melancholy stories there are that come to our ears.'

But one can only repeat: there are other ways of losing one's home and, with it, identity that are less dramatic but just as telling in their long-term effect. The writer Vladimir Nabokov, in his memoir *Speak, Memory*, when separated by decades, a distinguished career and several language shifts from his unvisitable past, wrote that he had fantasies of putting through an international call to the telephone number of his childhood home in St Petersburg. Would he just get the voice of the operator telling him, 'No such number … No such country'? Or would he hear the well-remembered voice of their long-standing manservant saying in Russian, 'My respects … '?

The experience of forced exile lurking behind this comforting dream has been a classic one of mid-twentieth-century Europe and shows every sign of continuing to haunt the world in the twenty-first, but the theme extends far back in time – '*By the waters of Babylon there we sat down and wept. Yeah, we wept when we remembered, O Sion.*'[25]

Such was the biblical lament of Jews exiled to slavery in Mesopotamia in an early dispersal more than two and a half thousand years ago, as they mourned for Jerusalem that was lost to them, far to the west. (There is still a site called Babylon in modern Mesopotamia, which is Iraq.) The concept of the Lost Country has marked Jewish history and Jewish thought, and sometimes the losses have been multiple. Jews ceased to weep, and settled down in Iraq as they did all over the Middle East. They created well-entrenched homes, in spite of the ritualistic Passover wish to be 'Next year in Jerusalem'. In the early decades of the twentieth century there may have been as many as forty thousand Jews spread through towns in Iraq: estimates vary, but the numbers were certainly significant. In the capital, Baghdad, it was said that more than 30 per cent of the population was Jewish. They did not erect social fences of strict orthodoxy around themselves, and lived on friendly terms with their Muslim and Christian neighbours, but they did not intermarry much: they were so numerous they presumably did not need to. By the 1930s Baghdad was a cosmopolitan and modern city, protected and defended from Nazi interests by Britain because of the all-important presence of oil. Iraqi Jews therefore survived the Second World War in something of a peaceful bubble. No Holocaust reached them there, any more than it did the Jews of neighbouring Iran, who had long ago survived the Babylonian attempt to exterminate them by prohibitions and assimilation, and had been reinstated by the Persians.[26] It was the post-war establishment of Israel and the consequent rise of Arab nationalism that spelt the beginning of the end for the age-old Jewish culture in these countries. A stealthy mass-exodus began. Like their German and Austrian co-religionists a generation earlier, these unwilling refugees had to leave most of their possessions behind, along with their houses and their identities. Today, in the whole of Baghdad, I am told, only five identifiable Jews remain.

Adults, however well adapted to a new life in Finchley, Altrincham or the outer suburbs of New York, never quite lose the accent of their original home. It is otherwise for children, especially for those who come so young, with minds so malleable and adaptable, that they lose instead the language and identity of their earliest years. Many of the Jewish children of the *Kindertransporten*, brought to safety in England in 1938 and 1939 by determined well-wishers who had realised the urgency of such action, carried precious, individual objects with them: a beloved soft toy, a pair of skates ... A few of these iconic possessions survive today in the Imperial War Museum. But one wonders how many of them retained a living meaning for their young owners, once several years had passed and a different life in England had replaced the old one? For the bigger children, memories remained and indeed became unnaturally fixed, iconic in themselves – but for those who had arrived off the Harwich boat-train at Liverpool Street Station at a very young age it was a different matter.

One who arrived, aged four, was fostered in the home of a kindly middle-aged couple, who treated him as if he were their own child. Six years later, when the Second World War ended, he had long become a happy English schoolboy, his infantile German quite forgotten. In 1945 the foster parents, mindful that Ernie (once Ernst)[27] was not necessarily theirs to keep, assured him, 'We'll start making enquiries through the Red Cross ... We'll try to find your parents ... We should soon have some news …' They meant so well that Ernie felt he could not tell them not to search, but in secret he hoped desperately that they would be unsuccessful. At ease in his new identity, he dreaded being sent 'home' to a galaxy of strange, foreign people with whom he would have nothing in common, not even language, and a wrecked country where terrible things had been going on.

In the event, his prayer was answered: it turned out that not a single one of his extensive birth family had survived. He grew up in Britain as an apparently well-balanced man, successful in a professional occupation. But to thrive by rejecting the past, however remote, must tend to leave a sense of guilt, even if it is never named as such. That past has become dangerous territory, a shadow-place not to be spoken of. The very small boy who, no doubt, had been fearful and probably tearful when he was put on a train by his desperate parents in the charge of older children must have suffered. But that boy was gone and the suffering wiped from conscious memory. It took Ernie most of a lifetime to tell even his wife how he had felt as a schoolboy at the war's end, and even longer to manage a brief visit to the German city where his earliest years were spent. Though the city had been much bombed by the end of the war, by a chance that many people might regard as lucky, the street and the actual apartment block where he had spent his infancy were still standing. He might have preferred it otherwise.

It must, I think, be abundantly clear, from this one inconspicuous example among a myriad of possible ones, that to suppress all memory of a lost past, lost love, may be the most effective and natural way of coping with it. And if this is the case when the destruction of all that one has known before has happened, so to

speak, offstage, how much more so when one has been a witness
to some brutal and terrible mechanism of loss?

The dilute Freudianism that has permeated our thinking on
such matters for most of the twentieth century, and still does
today, regularly favours what is known irreverently as the
'hydraulic' theory of the psyche. This is the notion that whatever
experiences go in must, at some point, be 'brought to the surface'
again, as if they were a volume of water that has to find a way
out and 'be expressed'. A large professional edifice of therapy
designed to achieve this end has been erected, and shows few
signs of being dismantled. Yet such clinical trials as have been
conducted on victims of physical and psychological traumas have
produced a different result from the one expected.[28] On the
whole, patients who were not encouraged to talk much about
what they had suffered fared better, psychologically, than those
who were invited to dwell on the matter. Common observation,
indeed, suggests that 'reliving' a terrible experience is not actually
how human beings cope, or ever have. When something truly
dreadful occurs (fill in your own most hideous example culled
from the world's news …) you cannot realistically 'come to terms
with it' or 'reframe it', nor should you. Your only salvation, the
traditional resort of generation upon generation of the oppressed
and tormented, is to put it behind you, blot it out and go on
living on whatever terms are manageable. And this seems to
apply equally to less obvious and dramatic losses.

Such, I came to realise long, long after the event, was the
solution resorted to by my brother.

Driven apart as we were by multiple circumstances while he, N,
was still a child, we got to know each other again to some extent

long after we were both adult, indeed in middle life. Trying, I suppose, to re-erect broken bridges to the past that was beyond recovery, I would every so often offer him some small piece of reminiscence, but the only sort that evoked any response in him were those to do with the country railway line. That, he remembered with affectionate detail and with the addition of adult expert knowledge ('Those were such-and-such-class tank engines, designed in 1911' – or whatever). But of the house where we lived till he was eight he seemed to recall absolutely nothing. Shown photos of its garden, where he had spent many happy hours pottering with toys and pet guinea pigs, he genuinely could not recognise it at all. Most adults will recall such a place from extreme youth, in part because it has become involuntarily their mental image of the Garden of Eden, however inappropriate. But N's Eden had apparently been wiped from memory. Nor could he recognise pictures taken in our Sussex grandparents' house or garden, where he had often played as well.

Given that this was someone who had such a good visual memory that, between the ages of three and four, he had acquired the ability to read simply by looking at the words in a book that was being read aloud to him, this failure was, to say the least, disconcerting.

I eventually noticed that he could not recognise photographs of our mother, either. Nor, seemingly, did he want to. I did not like to comment directly on this.

'In one year,' he said matter-of-factly to me once, 'I changed school, home and mother … What do you expect?'

It was, I realised with a sense of cold in the stomach, literally true. I had not, quite, put these three separately traumatic events together in my mind before.

It was evident that the steam-trains of his early childhood had become the single preserved, enshrined memory of happiness in a wilderness of loss that was beyond his nine-year-old power to examine, and had remained as such.

One quite other time, when I myself was distressed about something – the only meeting in our whole lives when our roles seemed to be reversed – he said to me, 'Remember: the past cannot hurt you.'

Regardless of the separate ways in which this statement is, and is not, true, I was struck by the conviction with which he stated it. And shrank from the thought of the level of suffering that must have led eventually to such a determined and stoic conclusion.

CHAPTER XI

The London in People's Minds

Sometimes, of course, the beloved habitat of childhood, youth or the prime of life is lost not by war, exile or personal tragedy, but by sheer population pressure and the need, or presumed need, to accommodate more and more people on previously unbuilt land. The spread of London is a theme that has already fleetingly appeared in this account. This is hardly surprising, as it has been a theme haunting social and architectural history for the last four centuries.

Already, by the time of Elizabeth I, there were anxieties about the capital city's insistent tendency to spread beyond the prescribed confines of her medieval walls and gates. Houses appeared beyond Whitechapel in the east, across the Fleet stream to the west, and northwards beyond the Bishop's Gate and at the Charterhouse at Smithfield. Edict upon edict was delivered, forbidding the erection of new houses within two miles of the walls – an early attempt to preserve London's integrity by creating a mini green-belt around it. But such strictures seemed to be unenforceable, no doubt in part because it tended to be

rich, influential men who chose to build new homes on the edge
of open countryside.

Desirable residences 'almost in the country' have indeed been
advertised in all the eras ever since, with the inexorable result
that the magic 'country' recedes that much further with every
building that is erected on its fringe. Because London, along
with Britain itself, has suffered no foreign invasion for almost a
thousand years, its walled-citadel character was *de facto* abandoned centuries before the continental cities demolished their
own defences. With the coming of the Civil War in the seventeenth century a belated attempt was made to build earthworks
around the capital, but they proved useless. The Restoration in
the latter part of the century, with its natural tendency to ally
the City with Westminster and Whitehall Palace, was soon after
followed by the Great Fire of 1666. After that, huge numbers
of the better-off citizens fled the ruined City for the newly
appearing western suburbs of Soho and St James's, never to
return.

To understand this profound difference between London and
the higher-density concentrated capitals of Europe, it is sufficient
to realise that, as late as 1870, Paris, encased behind newly built
but traditional-style fortifications, was being besieged (and presently invaded) by the Prussian army. At the same period London
was busy developing more and more distant suburbs than ever
before, with a new and proliferating semi-underground railway
(the Metropolitan and District Line) encouraging the whole
process along.

All cities, including Paris, have a tendency to grow outwards,
but the extraordinary growth of London from the end of the
Napoleonic Wars in the early nineteenth century right on

through the entire reign of Queen Victoria and into the twentieth century was something unprecedented in world history. Today it is a phenomenon in cities worldwide, from the USA to China, via Mexico, Africa and Indonesia. But London experienced it first, and was therefore the first to enact, however belatedly, some effective legislation against ever more expansion. The 1932 Town and Country Planning Act stopped the inexorable progress of urban sprawl in its tracks, before Bedford could be irretrievably linked with Brighton in one vast metropolitan area – a long-term prophecy by the seventeenth-century polymath William Petty, which at one point looked dangerously close to coming true.

Because the long century of London's unrestricted growth is now slipping from living human memory, most people do not realise how traumatic its effect must have been on the two or three generations that lived through it. People today frequently claim how much their own neighbourhood has changed since they were children, but, except in districts where gratuitous destruction took place in the post-Second World War period, their experiences of change have actually been slow and relatively benign, compared with those of their predecessors in the same districts. The fact is, if you were born, say, in about 1820, in one of the numerous separate old villages that at that point surrounded London proper – Islington and Hackney, Kentish Town, Paddington, Kensington, Chelsea, Parson's Green, Battersea, Peckham, Stepney – you were born into a flowery, rural environment, with the convenience of shops and inns already ribbon-developing along the main high road or village green, but with market gardens, fields with cows, patches of woodland and open streams only a brief walk away. Yet in most cases you were scarcely even into middle age when your desirable home village had turned by insidious degrees into a completely built-up, railway-crossed, soot-blighted urban district, fated for inevitable social decline as the grander inhabitants (once again) moved in search of literal fresh fields and pastures new. And so the pastures continued inexorably to retreat further and further out.

In Kentish Town late in the nineteenth century, when the mainline Midland Railway had, along with other lines, cut its way through the heart of the place, and the district was well known not for market gardens or even for genteel residences but for piano and organ factories, an old man was wheeled in a bath-chair down the grimy, high-walled narrow street that still went by the name Anglers Lane. He had difficulty realising that he was passing over the actual spot where, as a boy, he had bathed naked from the grassy, deserted banks of the River Fleet – by 1870 encased in a storm drain. In his incredulity at the total disappearance of the world of his youth, which was still so real in his mind, he was one of a multitude.

I have already mentioned that the decorative plate, valued and preserved in the Camp-Montague household because some forgotten forebear had once given it to another, looks like a 'fairing' from the days when fields began just off the Mile End Road. By the latter half of the nineteenth century the old hamlets of Bethnal Green, Stepney Green, Poplar and Bow had acquired such an established character as London's East End, perceived through the eyes of London further west as one monolithic, heavily built quarter of labour and poverty, that the old identities of these settlements were rapidly wiped from human memory. Yet that time was not so far distant. Even by the mid-century, when maps to celebrate London's expansion, complete with miniature pictures of prestigious buildings, were produced to celebrate the Great Exhibition of 1851, and Stepney was dense with terrace housing, Bow, further east again, was still largely unbuilt. But the London map I prefer is a little-known one, published (with touching precision) 'on January 1st 1818' in Paternoster Row. It captures exactly the moment when the lanes around Mile End Road and St Dunstan's Church by Stepney Green were becoming lined with houses. But the fields behind, which had been used for centuries for fairs, cattle-grazing, troop manoeuvres and rebellions, were still open to a sky not yet engulfed in London's smoke.

There are some other reasons why I prize this map, although it is by far the most modest and tattered of the fairly extensive collection of maps that has accumulated in our house over the last fifty years. For one thing, it shows a world on the very brink of change. Since 1800 the London Dock at Wapping had been constructed, with plans indicated on the map for other basins towards Shadwell. The 'Intended Line of the Regent's Canal' snakes around the whole of the eastern settlements near London from Islington and Hackney to distant Limehouse. The West India Docks still further east have also been opened, transforming for ever London's parameters. The classic working-class world of dockyard employment must have been gearing up to overwhelm the district. Yet Stepney still, just, had pretensions to gentility; there were some grand houses there occupied by well-to-do people who had not yet sold up and moved westwards or southwards. The parish had not acquired one of the new-built 'Waterloo churches' that were subsidised by the government to celebrate the defeat of Napoleon (there was one down the road at Shadwell). However, it had its own brand-new 'Trafalgar Square' off ancient White Horse Lane, to celebrate the earlier victory of Nelson against the French fleet.

Another reason I value this map is that both it and the little cardboard case into which it neatly folds to a pocket-sized shape are extremely battered and fragile. Its folds are threatening to split: disintegration hovers. It is clear that, uncoloured, it was never meant for hanging on the wall, but for busy use around London. I imagine that it belonged to some energetic man whose occupation – building surveyor? salesman? piano-tuner? Missionary to the Poor? – took him all over the expanding metropolis in those days a decade before the arrival of the first horse-drawn omnibus. In all the centuries before the slow and piecemeal evolution of public transport, ordinary people thought nothing of walking great distances, often daily, out of simple necessity.

A further reason this map means something to me is that it was given to me by someone who grew up in the East End, though more than a hundred years after the map was made, and lived for most of his childhood around the corner from Trafalgar Square, Stepney. By the 1930s all pretensions to grandeur had long vanished and it was a district of the poor. All Len's grandparents had arrived at various times from Eastern Europe or Russia, part of that substantial Jewish immigration that was to give the East End a further significant character, and most of the family laboured in one way or another in the garment trade. By the time of Len's birth in 1926 his parents and elder sister were living, along with a family of cousins, in a small house in Duckett Street off Trafalgar Square. It wasn't a predominately Jewish street, but there was a Jewish old people's home on nearby Stepney Green (by then reduced to a narrow grassy walkway with trees along it) and in the 1930s the area was on the route of Mosley's anti-Jewish Fascist marches. One of Len's childhood memories was of his mother responding rudely from an upper window to the speech-making Mosley. But it was basically a happy childhood, a world of neighbourliness and street games: the old villages had vanished in London's embrace as if they had never been, but communities felt well established and stable.

All this world, too, came to an end. Already, before the war, Len had won one of the rare free places then on offer at a grammar school; life was beginning to move him away from his origins. The move accelerated when the war came and he was evacuated to the country with his school. By the time he returned, a well-grown seventeen-year-old with plans for higher education, Duckett Street had been half-destroyed in the Blitz, the family were dispersed and his mother was soon to die of a disease that a few years later could have been successfully treated: this was just before the coming of the National Health Service.

Via an initial degree in engineering, a career that his headmaster had been keen for him to take up, Len eventually found his way to evening classes in singing and drama, and so onto the professional stage and a lifetime of varied satisfaction. For many years, art imitating life, he played the doctor in the television series *EastEnders*, who was supposed, like him, to have been a scholarship boy from a poor Jewish home. The doctor, it was indicated, had chosen to remain near his roots – though in practice the one-time East End had by then been so far destroyed that whether the doctor would still have felt at home either in the present-day reality or in the imaginary world conjured up by the scriptwriters seems questionable.

Len himself had by then moved far, socially and geographically, from Duckett Street. He retained fond memories of it, but had not been in that district for many years and did not really want to know whether or not the street was gone. One day when he was old and not very well, he visited our house and gave me the little 1818 map. 'I know you like these things,' he said. He had had it in his possession for most of his life, having been charmed as a young man at finding the remembered Trafalgar Square on it, new-built with no small streets as yet around it. (They were very soon to come.) He was due to go into a home for aged actors out on the rim of Greater London, which he shortly did. He was feeling the need to divest himself of many of his possessions, preferably to people who would appreciate them. '*We brought nothing into this world …* '

When people look at the East End today, still with its medieval street market along Whitechapel High Street, but with the giant glass-and-steel blocks looming from the encroaching City, or take a bus along Mile End Road to Bow, past acre after acre of banal post-war local-authority flats, they readily assume that most of what was there in the first decades of the twentieth century was destroyed in the famous Blitz of the Second World War. However, this was only true of certain streets and quarters. Over much of Whitechapel, Bethnal Green, Stepney, Mile End, Limehouse, Poplar and Bow, entire streets survived. Some were damaged beyond repair, but many were not. Most of the street patterns, created organically by the gradual process of urban growth, were still intact.

Essentially, the East End of London was transformed once again not by malevolent destruction, but by the ideologically driven conceit and lack of regard for ordinary people's lives and memories that possessed those in charge. As the maverick but distinguished architectural writer Ian Nairn put it in the 1960s, 'The East End was not destroyed by bombs; it has been broken on the planners' wheel.'

The comprehensive County of London Plan was drawn up even before the war was over. Essentially, although London had never been as densely populated as the continental capitals, there was an obsession with reducing the population of the East End for imprecisely defined 'health reasons'. The 'surplus population' was to be sent out to new towns that were designed to invade swathes of countryside with even less density. The separate local authorities, not yet amalgamated into the present-day large ones, adopted the Plan's principles with enthusiasm, scenting a fashionably left-wing modernity, plus a chance to get rid of a substantial portion of their rather turbulent population. There was also a genuine, if ill-thought-out belief that the poverty and vice of the past could only be eradicated by destroying the architecture of the past, as if the streets themselves were somehow responsible for classic urban ills.

There were references in this Plan of architectural amnesia to 'community spirit' and 'social group structures', but its lack of any real regard for such imponderables can be gauged by the fact that under the Plan one-third of Poplar and two-thirds of Stepney, a total of almost two thousand acres, were to be flattened and rebuilt. Moreover, the zones that were to be designated for 'homes' and those for 'open spaces' (the small industries that had been the life-blood of the East End hardly seemed to get a look-in) were allocated with extraordinary arbitrariness. Thus in the Stepney Green area, where the east side including Duckett Street and Trafalgar Square had been left largely in ruins because the German bombers had been aiming at gas-holders near there, many of the streets of small houses to the west of the church survived more or less intact. Logic might have suggested that the much-heralded Open Space should be laid out in the devastated area and people's homes elsewhere rehabilitated. Yet when I was visiting clients of Stepney Old People's Welfare Association as late as 1963, twenty years after the worst of the bombing, all these streets of mainly solid little houses, which merely needed to have their roofs mended and bathrooms installed on the back, were 'scheduled for demolition'. So determined was the Borough of Stepney about this that it routinely refused to sanction external repairs to such houses, even at a landlord's own expense.

The mantra of the old ladies, and occasional old gentleman, that I visited, in their small front rooms with clocks and china dogs and bobbled fringes on the mantelpieces, was the same: 'It's all coming down round here, darlin'.' It was said not with the interest or excitement that those in charge of the Borough of Stepney hoped to generate for their Brave New World of high-rise flats, but with an apprehensive acceptance. The people in the surviving small houses had been led to believe this upheaval was inevitable, but they felt hurt in a profound, inarticulate way at what was being done, at the zero-value accorded to the very fabric of their lives. The dismantling of old neighbourhoods had been going on for years, and it had already been noticed that you might get sent to live miles from your familiar grounds ('decanted' was the word used), with no guarantee at all that you would ever be returned. 'And what about my rabbits?' one man asked me. What, indeed? Rabbits were considered to have no place in modern living. Many people too were told to have their dogs and cats destroyed, with the threat (always implicit, if rarely actually stated) that unless they did so, they would not be offered new accommodation.

Of course the destruction of human lives was never anywhere in the minds of the council officials who enacted these Soviet-style procedures. They believed, on the contrary, that they were embarked on an essentially moral crusade. However, it seems worth making the point that the sweeping-away of homes and whole districts, and hence the desecration of memories, has been a traditional aspect of oppression in place after place, century after century.

Inexorably, the corrugated-iron screens went up in small street after small street, leaving only public houses and the occasional chapel isolated on corners – for whom, one wondered, since their customers and congregations were being dispersed far and wide? A woman I met many years later remembered the time well: 'Every weekend another neighbour or other was leaving. People who came to see them off used to cry. Each time it was like a funeral. There was nothing you could do about it.'

In fact, by the mid-1960s, things were beginning to be 'done', in the form of highly critical articles in the better-informed sections of the press. Post-war doctrines about the State knowing what was best for its citizens were at last being questioned, on the political Left as well as the Right. It was noticed that many of the new housing developments were engendering their own patterns of poverty and vice, becoming in effect the new slums.

Articles in popular magazines were no longer about a shining future full of radiant towers ('streets in the sky'), but had titles such as 'An Indictment of Bad Planning'. Such journalism annoyed the entrenched planners considerably, but it was indeed prophetic. Today, many of the unlovable tower-blocks that replaced the old street patterns of the East End have, in turn, been demolished.

It had also become apparent by the 1960s that in London districts where some of the population was rather better educated than most East Enders, a considerable fight-back had already begun. With the abandonment of steam-trains on the railways, and of open fires in favour of central heating, inner London was cleaner than it had been for a hundred years. As a result, many of the dilapidated Georgian and early Victorian districts that the Plan had dismissed as 'inchoate areas ripe for removal' – usually for converting into moral-sounding Green Spaces – had become the lovingly restored and fiercely defended territory of a new generation of home-owners. A Labour Minister of Housing[29] complained, along with the usual references to 'rat-infested slums', that 'Old terrace houses may have a certain snob-appeal to members of the middle class but they are not suitable accommodation for working class tenants.' The Minister in question came from a privileged background: the overall contempt that his remark betrayed, apparently for the whole range of his fellow-citizens, was noted and was not forgiven.

The delusion that arbitrary redevelopment could transform life itself and human nature was not, of course, confined to London. Stepney, and a particular corner of it on an ancient map, is just one specific example of the mass-planning delusion that wrecked large towns all over the United Kingdom.

In many places, far from the influence of vociferous architectural writers and conservationists, the message concerning the psychological and social destruction wrought by high-handed, large-scale schemes took decades more to penetrate. In a few places it has barely been absorbed even today. Manchester, Liverpool and Glasgow suffered far more comprehensively than London did, and Birmingham was subjected to the profound character-change of having major motor-roads driven right through its centre – a fate that London managed to avoid, by public outcry.

The Greater London Plan, the successor to the County of London Plan, was predicated on the notion that the dominance of private cars was where the future of all large cities lay, almost as if this was not so much a choice as a law of nature. It announced a series of concentric ringroads to be carved out through densely built areas of inner London. But very fortunately, by the time this Plan was unveiled in the mid-1960s to an incredulous populace, it came some ten or fifteen years too late. Public opinion was by then sufficiently well informed and well mobilised to fight.

After the bruising and increasingly costly experience of building one relatively short section of urban motorway between the Edgware Road and Shepherd's Bush (the 'Westway') – and blighting and fragmenting a whole district in the process – the recently-formed Greater London Council had to concede defeat. The physical correlate to London-in-the-mind, that enormous memory bank for millions, many of them scattered across the world, was not going to be comprehensively destroyed after all.

CHAPTER XII

A House. And a Map

We know that Blanche Jacob, my paternal grandmother, was a hoarder of letters. Among the vast collection of these kept by her and by Bertie, which turned up quite unexpectedly in a barn they had never seen, long after both were dead, I came across two from myself.

I think, from the evidence of these scant missives, that one must have been written in the spring of 1943 and the other later the same summer. Already a passionate if incompetent drawer of pictures, I was not yet five nor at any sort of school and could not effectively write. But I seem to have known my letters (in capitals, as that was how the alphabet was then usually taught), and therefore could laboriously write down each letter of a message at a drunken angle when it was named by my mother. In the first missive I am thanking Granny for 'the shredded wheat' and in the second for a pot of jelly. The cereal would have come from the modern factory in the equally modern (and resented) Welwyn Garden City, which had invaded my grandparents' rural Hertfordshire seclusion between the wars. The jelly was probably home-made redcurrant, produce of their large garden. I know that my mother and I had stayed with them for a week sometime before, en route between one transient wartime abode and another. The visit wasn't, I surmise, a great success. They decided I was 'spoilt' (the criticism-of-refuge of all inexperienced grandparents). Their self-opinionated daughter-in-law was not really the person they would have wished their cherished son to marry. She and Blanche were, I suspect, covert enemies from the outset. But I believe they were both trying hard.

It now seems a telling historical comment on the privations of wartime Britain that a small child would really be pleased by presents of breakfast cereal and jam, but I think that I was: I remember the novelty of shredded wheat with a vague aura of pleasure. But the only personal significance of these communications is that each of them contains artwork. The shredded-wheat one is decorated with a very approximate picture of 'MY HOUSE', which was a small one in Sussex near to my other, better-known and beloved grandparents, into which my mother and I had recently moved. I seem to have noted, with selective precision, the roof timbers, the front steps and one large window. Plus a railway line. The rather later jelly-letter proclaims 'THIS IS A MAP', alongside an uneven patch of green with a blue line alongside it. No designation is given. But I know that it is a small section of Ashdown Forest, open heathland really, with a stream through it, which had become the joy of my life that summer and was to remain so for several years.

What strikes me about these two unremarkable, baby thank-you letters is the way they exemplify two of the themes, houses and intimately known places, that have turned out to be important in my life and in my work. Someone must have shown me a map and explained what it was, and a lifetime's love-affair with cartography was born, but I do not know who this person was. It would not have been my mother, who was one of that large number of women who 'can't read maps'. She tended not to look at them anyway, because she disliked putting on her glasses. And at the moment when I drew this, my first map, of a small green valley in Ashdown Forest, my father – who did rather like maps – was a completely unknown figure to me, as he had been away on military service in the Middle East since 1939. A typical wartime childhood. School, when I eventually reached it, had plenty of other children whose fathers were unknown or barely remembered uniformed figures scattered in foreign places. None of us thought this was odd; we were too young to have prejudices in the matter. The war was a fact of life and seemed to us quite a logical one, a classic contest between goodies and baddies. 'Before the war' – that lost country that grown-ups went on about – was outside our memories.

As to the house pictured on the first letter, the vagaries of war and evacuation had taken my mother and me to several different places, and I feel that the phrase 'a home of our own' (though I think the Sussex cottage was rented) had considerable resonance for me, as it did for her. I recall her telling me, before we left a shared house in Reading, 'When we have a home of our own we'll have it decorated as we like.' She must have meant distempered walls and perhaps personally chosen curtain material (most of my parents' previous possessions, stored in London, had disappeared under a bomb in 1940, and some statutory payout was due to them). But to me the word 'decorations' conveyed home-made Christmas paper-chains and – if one was lucky – some hoarded 'pre-war' spangly things, and I was a little disappointed that these did not materialise. However, our new home-of-our-own was more eccentrically interesting than it seemed from its prim front, for the man who had constructed it as his own habitat many years before had his special priorities. At the back was a range of sheds full of interestingly derelict bits of machinery, and you could climb onto the shed roofs via a conveniently placed quince tree. There was also, encircling the sitting room, a conservatory with a grapevine and a mimosa. The antiquated boiler in the side-wall that should have kept them continually warm was, of course, unused in those times of chronic coal shortages, but they seemed to flourish all the same, especially the mimosa with its powdery-yellow blossoms, which I thought then, and still think, heart-breakingly beautiful. My toy-farm animals ('pre-war' and second-hand, since one could by then buy very few toys) basked under this beauty, surrounded by hopefully planted tomatoes.

My mother, and my father when he finally came back from the war, via Italy and then Normandy, regarded the conservatory as 'insufferably Victorian'. When they were negotiating to purchase the house, I seem to recall they had plans to demolish all that glass. But the plan was abandoned. After my brother's birth we moved instead to the rather larger house not far from the railway line, but in a more isolated situation. This, for social reasons that were never quite expressed, was perceived as more desirable. It had a large garden (I think my father, accommodating with difficulty to marriage again after such a long break and so much unshared experience, was reaching wistfully back to his Hertfordshire childhood), but I can now see that this other house was amazingly ill-designed. Although it dated only from the 1930s, I believe it had been constructed by a local builder without benefit of an architect. It was cramped where it should not have been, space-wasting in other parts, with its fireplaces meanly sited in corners and the whole building orientated the wrong way. In an inept attempt to give the exterior an old-world, dormer look, the bedroom windows on the first floor were placed too high for anyone to look out of them. Whether my schoolchild self did register all these defects in a subliminal way – I was now amusing myself by drawing plans of imaginary dwellings – or whether my mother's emotional decline and fall during the years in this house have in any case cast a retrospective pall over the whole place for me, I cannot now judge. All I do know is that the first little house, the one near Ashdown Forest, has come back to me at long intervals, even now after so many decades, in dreams of rare sweetness, whereas the interior of the second one, though remembered in prosaic detail, seems to have vanished from my subconscious as completely as it did from my brother's conscious memory-store.

Ten years after that second house was abandoned, and our mother abandoned life, and our shocked father abandoned various other priorities by diving too quickly into a new and ill-considered marriage, I was married myself. In those long-lost days of cheap, if rather dilapidated housing, we soon bought the inner-London house in which we still live, more than fifty years later. It is slightly unusual these days to have lived in one house for so long, as our ancestors often did, passing a farm or an old house in a provincial town from generation to generation. I sit writing this in the room where I gave birth to our son a lifetime ago, while his own elder son, now a grown man in turn, is bedded down temporarily in the room where his father was conceived, though I have not mentioned that to him.

Most houses of a certain age are, in any case, silently packed with other families' past loves, pains, griefs, pleasures, reunions and regrets, with childbirths and deaths, vibrating eternally perhaps on a wavelength inaccessible to us. For in most cases all this lived time is beyond our ken, nothing to do with us, irretrievable – except for this single, odd, strong bond: we are living in these strangers' space. We are occupying the same square footage of floor, looking out of the same windows, running up the same stairs with our hands on the turn of the bannister rail at just the same opportune place as all the hands that have preceded us. Arguably, we are closer to them, in all their intricate daily living, than we are to some remote great-grandparent we have located by Internet research, who lived in a distant city where we have never been.

'Land and houses,' says a Hindu proverb, 'have their own destiny.' And houses, which we only borrow for our own span, live longer than people, often much longer. Evidently there is something specific about the destiny of our particular modest-sized house because, unlike most of its fellows in the streets of north London, it has actually been home to a relatively small number of families. In another decade, as I write this, it will be two hundred years old. And yet, apart from some early, transient tenants, it has sheltered only five sets of owner-occupiers, each set for a great swathe of years.

The section of land where the house and its adjoining ones have stood since 1828, just off a very ancient route northwards, formed part of the land previously attached to a long-established country ale-house. By the late eighteenth century these grounds had become the tea-garden and bowling green of what was by then a fashionable coaching inn, a pleasant place to drive, ride or walk out to from London town on a Sunday. What had been for many centuries a modest village of dairy farmers, remote from urban life, was beginning to become a flowery suburb where genteel people took lodgings in the summer months. But the same influences that made the public-house garden desirable as a place of relaxation also made it an increasingly marketable commodity. Sections of it fronting a footpath, which led to a stile and a byway to Islington, began to be sold off for the construction of gentlemen's villas. One of these gentlemen, having bought a sizeable plot, later donated part of his garden for a chapel to be built.

By the time the Napoleonic War was over and a post-war building boom got going, the mounting value of the remaining public-house land was evidently too tempting to resist. In an arrangement that was slightly unusual (most houses were then leasehold, being built in large estates by speculative developers) the bowling green was sold off mainly in small freehold lots to individual purchasers. In 1824 a Mr Crowe rented a plot for one year and then bought it. By 1828 he had built on it a house – now ours – which was very slightly more elegant than the conjoined one put up by the buyer of the next-door plot: it had front-steps. Its façade was only twenty-five feet wide, but its back garden, of the same width, stretched two hundred and thirty feet, all the way to the ancient far wall of what had been the inn's gardens.

Both houses and the several others that adjoined them were 'intended to form a new street called Gloucester Place', but, like the country dwelling that it still in spirit was, Crowe's house was given a wide entrance hall with graceful stairs leading out of it. It had only a single upper storey and no basement, and it had no mains drainage system, either. Water seems to have been supplied by a pump outside the back door, presumably tapping off a pipe from the Highgate reservoirs that passed down through Kentish and Camden Town en route to Bloomsbury. The only privy was an earth-closet at the back, beyond the wash-house and coal-store. Every so often men would come with barrows, empty the privy and trundle the contents down to the end of the garden, where they were deposited through an aperture in the old wall of the bowling green into a cart waiting in the field behind. It would be fifteen years before the road in front that had replaced the footpath acquired a mains sewer running beneath it. After that house-owners were invited – though not obliged – to get linked up to the system. However, it was 1858 before the owner of this particular house joined forces with the owner of the next-door property to share the cost of a drain connection. There is some suggestion in the drainage documents of that time that the parish authorities, pushed to it by a recent Metropolitan Local Act, were now of the view that a proper drain and a water-closet (even if still in the yard) were really a necessity.

The deeds show that in 1840 the house had been acquired from Mr Crowe by a Henry Hugh Pike, aged about thirty, barrister-at-law. (Mr Crowe was now living in Sussex and styling himself 'gentleman', presumably on the proceeds of successful building ventures.) Mr Pike claimed then to be a member of Lincoln's Inn, though it was actually Gray's Inn where he had qualified for the Bar – an odd misstatement that turns out to have been rather typical of him. He bought the house for £900, then a substantial sum of money, which must have reflected the continuing desirability of the neighbourhood. But presumably he intended it as an investment and a source of income, for he did not live there. In the following year it was occupied by a 'widow of independent means' with a couple of servants; and by the Census of 1851 the tenant was a young architect, his wife, a servant, a monthly nurse and two children, one of whom was a newborn baby – the first birth to take place in one of the three bedrooms, I think, but far from the last.

By the Census of 1861, Pike was actually living in the house, along with his wife, four daughters (ages ranging from twelve to four) and a son of two. Unlike most of their neighbours, the family employed no live-in servant girl. This hardly suggests prosperity, and indeed Pike must have been in difficulties for some years, since in 1844 he had been disbarred from his profession. When I discovered this I hoped that he might have committed some flamboyant offence, but it turned out that he had merely been involved in the then-rather-common misdemeanour of associating too closely with a solicitor and presumably colluding with him over the proceeds from a case. Now styling himself 'retired', Pike was ostensibly cultivating vegetables and chickens in his lengthy garden, but by 1866 he was embroiled in a row with several of his immediate neighbours. He brought a case against them for trespass and conspiracy, with evidence on both sides so unseemly and ridiculous that when the matter came to court, it was made the subject of a condescendingly humorous article in the *Daily Telegraph*.[30] Accusations concerning 'impudent looks', insults, dead chickens, squibs and crackers, damaged vegetables, dirty water, imitations of a pig and a crowing cock, and 'sitting on the garden wall drinking and smoking', flew back and forth. There was also a further, odder accusation, concerning a dead mackerel put up on a pole outside Pike's door with the inscription 'Beware the Pike – he is a most voracious fish.' Can Pike, I wonder, have tried to keep going by using what capital he had to set up as a money-lender? If so, he hardly succeeded, and his children were said by one neighbour to be 'starved, uneducated and ill-clothed'.

Faced with this saga, the court simply bound over all parties to keep the peace.

The area was still moderately respectable; the chief participants in the Pike affair were a commercial traveller, a prominent local builder and their wives. But a mainline railway (the Midland into St Pancras) had arrived just down the road, new terraces were going up in all directions, and the place was no longer the pretty suburb surrounded by fields that it had been when Pike had bought the house more than twenty-five years before. In spite of this, and of whatever financial vicissitudes he was passing through, he was not deterred some four years later from extending his house. The kitchen stove and chimney were repositioned. The back bedroom above was rebuilt with a high ceiling, and was extended into what must have been intended to be an impressive upstairs room for daytime use. The transformation was completed with a fine marble fireplace in this room, too grand for the general style of the house, and a huge north-facing window.

To support this new structure, a very solid end-beam was put in place. The workmen who uncovered this beam a hundred years later, when the young couple who were my husband and me were having further works done on the kitchen, judged it to be of mahogany and far older than the house itself. Mahogany is a tropical hardwood native to the Americas. It began to be imported into Europe from the time of the Spanish conquests, and then in greater quantities from the Caribbean islands in the seventeenth and eighteenth centuries, when it was prized for ships' timbers. The architect who inspected our beam said that he thought this immensely tough piece of our home had probably sailed the seas for a good many years, absorbing salt, before it fetched up in some broker's yard down the Thames in the days when wooden ships were being replaced by iron and steel, and had been bought up by a London builder. So this part of our house had, and has, a further secret history much, much longer than that of its transient dwellers.

It was presumably for these substantial works that in 1870 Henry Hugh Pike took out a mortgage on the house. (He was now, according to the document in the deeds, styling himself 'solicitor'.) What on earth did he have in mind for this new construction? A music room, a studio … ? Could he have been planning to run one of those tiny private schools that abounded in Victorian towns?

It is evident that Pike considered himself a highly moral person. Underneath the floorboards of the new room, when they were disturbed a hundred years later, Temperance tracts appeared in profusion. It was also in 1870 that Pike (on that day signing himself 'formerly barrister-at-law') wrote to the local paper to complain about a newly constructed local church, both because gas light had been installed in it (unchristian?) and because its services were 'Romish'. But all these pretensions were of no avail. In 1880 the mortgage was foreclosed: the debt, swollen with unpaid interest, amounted to £400. The house was sold. Although it had been enlarged with the new upstairs room, and its big garden was still intact – longer by now than those of most along the terrace, whose back-land had been sectioned off by new cross-streets – at sale the property fetched only £500, as against the £900 it had been worth forty years before. Whatever else Pike was, he was clearly not a successful schemer.

When I first wrote about Pike, more than forty years ago, I regarded his story, complete with the newspaper cutting I had found about him, mainly as opportune comic relief in a book about urban development.[31] But over the years the elements of simple misery implicit in his tale began to sadden me. I did not want to think that we were sharing our personal space with the shadows of a family suffering so from anger and thwarted dreams. Beneath the low-class comedy in the preposterous row with the neighbours – the Pike family were counter-accused of having frequently addressed one neighbour's wife as 'beast' and 'Old Scraggy' – this is a sad tale, especially when you hear that during this saga one of the Pike children happened to die. In which bedroom, I can't help wondering?

High up near the landing on the otherwise elegant wooden hand-rail of the curving bannisters there is a deep-scored mark like a scar. I have wondered if, in some fit of temper between themselves, Mr or Mrs Pike had lashed out with some dangerous household implement. Or struggled clumsily, with loud recriminations, in getting a piano upstairs to the new room?

In the 1970s I had no obvious means of finding out who had lived in the house after the Pikes were finally forced to leave it – which they only seem to have done, rather oddly, sometime after the enforced sale. But with each new decade another instalment of past Census returns becomes available for general scrutiny, so now a whole other family has become part of the unseen, accreted presences within our home. These are a clan called Quilter, who seem, happily, to have been as different as possible from the Pikes.

Unlike the disbarred barrister, the Quilters appear to have had no social pretensions. Nor, by that time, had Kentish Town. What had originally been a polite Methodist chapel several doors along, with a pillared front, was now a Poor Law Relief Station and soup-kitchen. But in the house attached to ours on the other side there came to live, in the 1880s, a retired coach-painter and sign-painter who had clearly done well at his skilled trade and invested wisely, since he was 'living on own means'. It was presumably he who suggested to his son, who had followed him into the trade, that the house next door would be a good buy. At all events, in 1887, Eldred Quilter bought it for £500. It would not be sold for another thirty-nine years, and for all that time most of the extended Quilter family seem to have been living in it, apparently harmoniously. By a fine irony, Henry Pike's large, light back room with its engraved marble fireplace designed for a lofty purpose almost certainly became the sign-painting workshop. Every so often today, when one of the shops in the high road is being renovated, a sign finely painted in cursive, *trompe-l'oeil* style is briefly uncovered. I like to think that was Quilter work, the trade that kept our house warm and comfortable.

Even if the sign-business had not been flourishing, which it clearly was, by the years before the First World War the sum of money coming weekly into the household must, by the unassuming standards of skilled artisan life, have been substantial. Living in it in 1911 were Eldred Quilter, aged by then sixty-one ('sign writer on own account'), his wife, a married son who was employed elsewhere in a tailoring business, *his* wife, their two small daughters and two younger unmarried sons. One of these sons was a clerk in the East India Company office and the other an architect's assistant in the London County Council, which had been formed ten years before: good white-collar jobs, routes to a more middle-class existence. For the time being, however, this apparently harmonious family still adhered to the working-class habit of filling every room. If we exclude the kitchen (where everyone presumably ate meals together, and took turns in the wash-house behind), the big workroom above it and the front parlour that was obligatory for self-respect, that leaves one back room downstairs for the elders to share as a bedroom, an upstairs one for the unmarried sons, the front bedroom for the married couple and a very small one partitioned off the landing for their little girls. Propriety and gentility were thereby maintained, and I am sure no one wanted for anything.

In addition, the Quilters were proud of their house, and were not without up-to-date ideas for it. In 1903 the drain connection installed by Mr Pike (but apparently not in the proper place, as indicated on the plans some forty-five years before) was judged defective and was replaced by a better-placed one, no doubt with the encouragement of the recently established London County Council. In the front parlour the Quilters removed the narrow Georgian fire-grate and its overmantel (examples of which survive to this day upstairs) and replaced it by a more modern grate, with a proper tray for the ashes, dark-red tiling all round and a mantelpiece with side-shelves for displaying ornaments. They also embellished the large front hall with an example of early Art Deco paper – which saw the light again briefly about a century later, when the house, having lost its supporting terrace-companions on one side, needed underpinning.

But although indoor lavatories and even bathrooms were now commonplace in the ordinary houses that went on being built in those Edwardian years, as London expanded ever further out into the fields of Hornsey and Finsbury Park, it did not apparently occur to the Quilters to install one. They were no doubt used to their way of life, and comfortable with it – and where, anyway, would they have put a bathroom?

There had been a brief St Pancras Borough scheme c.1900 to build a public bathhouse, laundry and swimming pool on the site of the ex-Poor Law Relief Station next door. That would surely have been convenient for the Quilters. But in the end the bathhouse got built (in lavish Art Nouveau style) elsewhere in the district, and the Poor Law Guardians used some of their old site to build a new, modern, red-brick orphanage.

Eldred Quilter died, in his late seventies, in 1926, followed by his widow in 1931. It was only then that their youngest son Henry, whose proper baptismal name turns out on a document to be Herbert (no wonder he preferred Henry) and who still worked for the LCC, sold the house at last. It changed hands for £1,000, which by this time was worth only a little more than the £500 for which it had been sold in the 1880s.

It was acquired by a local medical practice and became the surgery of one of the partners, a Dr Pelly. Gas lighting had arrived in the house at some point, probably during the Pike decades; now electricity belatedly replaced it. And at last a bathroom, complete with WC, plus cupboards to contain water-tanks, was achieved by partitioning off a section of the big upstairs room that for so long had been a workroom. Its grandiose marble fireplace ended up oddly placed in a corner, where it remains to this day, a bathroom being too useful to remove.

One morning in 1970 I emerged from our house into the sunlight to post a letter in the box opposite and was confronted by a small old lady. She was bobbing about where our wrought-iron front gate must once have been, before it was removed in the Second World War on the pretext of making armaments.

Long explanation – she hardly ever came to Kentish Town these days … Just by chance here today … My sister, you see … Tulse Hill … Buses taking so long … Some shopping … Couldn't resist while she was here, coming along just having a look … So many years … Hope I didn't mind? … The Dear Doctor's house, you see …

Since she was clearly longing to see inside, I invited her in.

Did I remember Dr Pelly? No, of course I was too young … *Such* a good doctor. Took such care. And everyone knew him … He was the police surgeon, too, you see … Oh-oh! [By this time she was in the front downstairs room, the one-time parlour, which we had made our small son's playroom.] Oh – toys! Children! The Dear Doctor would be so pleased …

I was naturally gratified to hear that she thought us suitable to cohabit with the distinguished shade who occupied the house for ever, as far as she was concerned. Upon questioning, she revealed that the front room had been the waiting room (we might have guessed that, from the hard-wearing lino tiles that covered the floor) and that the back room had been the surgery. We might have guessed that, too, for it had acquired a little alcove built out into the yard, and there, beneath the window, was a washbasin. Very convenient for us, as at that time we had a friendly lodger-cum-babysitter renting that room.

What griefs, physical pains, despairs, but also, apparently, reliefs and encouragements, must that space have been a party to, in its surgery days.

The lady was disappointed, though hardly surprised given her own apparent age, to hear that the Dear Doctor was long dead. He had died after the Second World War, bequeathing the house to his housekeeper, whom I will call Mrs Welby, and her husband. We knew this, as they were the elderly couple from whom we had bought the house for £5,000 in 1963. They were moving out to the Great Cambridge Road, which they thought would be A Nicer Area, but 'I'm sure you'll be happy in the house, dear,' Mrs Welby had said. 'It's a lovely house, isn't it? We've been happy here.'

Their happiness had evidently consisted of painting all the woodwork chocolate-brown ('Doesn't show the dirt'), with the exception of the front bedroom, where they had indulged themselves with pinky-mauvish paint and wallpaper with Chianti bottles on it. Similarly the kitchen, where they seem to have lived full-time, was beautified with pea-green paint and wallpaper covered in large lilac blossoms. We abolished the wallpapers before we even moved in, but areas of serviceable chocolate and ebullient green still hide inside cupboards more than fifty years after the Welbys' departure. I think kindly of the Welbys and of their faint but gentle presence among all the other shadowy representatives of past times.

And I am conscious that we, too, though still tramping about over the intimately known old floorboards and calling to one another up and down the stairs, are representatives of another time. Our ideas of furnishing, of pictures, of the level of comfort we require, are those of our generation, not of today, and are poignantly dated, in the eyes of our grandchildren. After more than fifty years fitting snugly into our habitat, painting and papering its walls, using the limited number of rooms variously for different forms of work, and cooking innumerable meals for all sorts of people in traditional ways, the house has inevitably become something of a monument to us and our era. But this, too, will pass.

It could so easily have happened otherwise. Countless houses of this age, all over London and other large cities, have become nothing but rubble, dust, air and a perishing memory. Like a pack of old letters or theatre programmes, a battered medieval shoe or a Roman brooch, only by a series of almost random chances has this particular house survived.

Its two neighbours on one side were pulled down in the 1900s to create a driveway to the orphanage building that was superseding the old Poor Law Relief Station. How easily our house might have been included in the plan, if the arbitrary lines had been drawn a little differently! How easily too it might have fallen prey, as so many other houses did elsewhere in the immediate area, to post-Second World War plans for destroying homes to create a notionally healthier habitat while turning the inhabitants out. The subsequent Greater London Plan for a series of concentric motorway ringroads, complete with feeder roads to them and car parks at strategic points, was similarly drawn with the careless amplitude of view that characterised the State-knows-best ethos of that time.

I have an elusive but persistent memory that sometime in the mid-1960s I glimpsed a Plan that indicated just such an extensive car park, with a new elevated road snaking southwards from it, obliterating this entire terrace of houses and gardens. But no such horrors had appeared in the routine search made by a solicitor when we were buying the house. Perhaps this scheme was a last-gasp fantasy produced by an embattled road-designer. Or perhaps it is a false-memory, a night-terror of my own production. If places matter very much to you, that is what you dream about.

CHAPTER XIII

Memories Are Made of This

Memory, and in particular the fallibility of memory, has today become something of a fashionable subject. One has to agree that memory is obviously selective, that much is readily transposed, simplified or recalled over time with altered emphasis – which is not to say that the reworked memory is necessarily a less valid version of what originally happened than the immediate memory was. Sometimes it can turn out more essentially focused.

There is no doubt that this is a marshy area, and one where people tend to line up on different sides of the marsh. On one side there is a demand, which some people regard as unrealistic, but which is a main prop of court evidence and of legal systems, that a witness should strive to remember accurately actions, conversations, faces even, months or years after an event. And on the other side there is no shortage of psychologists or performers of magic tricks whose sincerely held conviction is that human memory is profoundly fallible and that we are

constantly reinventing the disordered and unstable contents of
what we assume to be our memory-store.

A further complicating view is added by the proponents of
what was announced twenty-five to thirty years ago, with a good
deal of publicity, as 'recovered memory syndrome', but is now
more often referred to as 'fake memory syndrome'. There do
remain fervent believers in the reliability of 'forgotten' memories
apparently recovered by psychoanalysis or hypnosis. They take
the view, in itself uncontroversial, that many people have buried
distressing memories deeply, inaccessible to everyday recall.
However, the energy with which some believers pursue these
invisible memories, with a pronounced emphasis on those that
might relate to sexual abuse in childhood, has led to the situation known to less gullible or merely more cynical observers as
the Freudian Trap: if you think you've managed to recall some
murky childhood event, that proves the validity of recovered
memory, whereas if you fail to do so, that just proves further
how deeply traumatised you must have been by the experience.
Then follow accusations, which by definition cannot be substan-
tiated. In such over-adherence to a questionable hypothesis,
genuine memories have been distorted, relationships wrecked
and families torn apart.

I will simply say that common observation suggests that the
extent and accuracy of memory-capacity varies very much from
one person to another, a fact that sometimes seems to be overlooked. Moreover, there are many different fields of memory,
with individuals excelling or performing feebly in various fields
according to their mental make-up. A very few people have an
extraordinary ability to recognise faces only fleetingly seen,
perhaps in a crowd, sometimes years before, and such an

exceptional skill is internationally prized by police forces for the help it can give in tracking down suspect individuals and their associates. At the other extreme, some people with capacious oral memories readily retain material from literature, films, lectures, broadcasts or conversations, yet have a genuine and embarrassing lifelong difficulty in recognising faces, even those of people they have met and talked to more than once. Some of them also have difficulty in learning to read.

I speak from personal experience. In the first school I attended, it was soon mistakenly believed I could read, when I could not: that was a skill I was painfully slow to acquire. What I had in fact done, without especially meaning to, was absorb by heart all the available reading-book passages through hearing other children read them aloud. I believe I thought that reciting a passage appropriately was what 'reading' meant. I was rather surprised when the head teacher, having been misled by my performance, seemed cross with me, though she was also slightly apologetic at having landed me in too high a class. 'A child like you – you'll soon catch up,' she said. It took me years, and much subterfuge.

There also appears to be a remarkably wide variation in how far back into infancy lasting memory extends, with some other-wise alert people seemingly unable to recall anything much of their early years, while others have a small store of precise and verifiable memories dating back to toddlerhood. A degree of fossilisation has probably set in here, but what are fossils if not an example of genuine preservation? Some of my own memories, such as playing naked in my grandparents' garden in a summer when I must have been just two and the grass tickled as I squatted down, I cannot in all honesty recall with the clarity and authenticity that I once could. But I know that the memory (validated also by a photograph) is essentially correct because, three years later, rediscovering the same garden in more coherent childhood, my earlier experience came back to me with a sense of remembered happiness. It thereby became fixed, creating a permanent record in my mind's store.

Evidence suggests that the human mind-store is often very extensive, and that for much of our busy lives we do not venture far into it, rather like someone in a family house with huge old attics, who goes up there only occasionally to retrieve suitcases or Christmas decorations and ignores the accreted piles of bygone possessions. Rare indeed is the human being like the much-studied Russian Solomon Shereshevsky (1886–1958) whose gift and misfortune were that he memorised everything, apparently without the wish to do so and without limit to his capacity, and retained all this hoarded material indefinitely. He was unable to block unwanted memories, or to understand abstract concepts or figurative language, or indeed literature in general. Evidently his lumber-stuffed mental attic was perpetually all around him, a kind of prison.

The great majority of people, more fortunate, have only occasional and fleeting access, most commonly in dreams, to this daunting storehouse. Once in my life, following a major operation and consequent doses of morphine, I found myself dreamily inhabiting my own attic of discarded memories, which was far larger than I had ever realised, full of previously forgotten people and interesting and intricate, if trivial, details. I rather enjoyed being in there for a few days, but do not expect to return to it. Unless indeed death turns out to be a brief, confused climb up a hitherto-hidden staircase to find an entire life at the top of it, a timeless wealth of recognition and recall.

There is, of course, a need to forget: the alternative, exemplified by poor Shereshevsky, is not encouraging. One may also take the utilitarian view that each generation must, of necessity, discard some part of the accumulated cultural memory of the previous one in order to make room for fresh mental baggage. This can be regarded as a version of 'the rubbish cycle', in which once-valued objects decline in perceived value till, regarded as worthless, they are mostly thrown away. Only after this general disposal and annihilation do the few examples that have somehow survived gradually reacquire a rarity interest and, therefore, value.

This obsolescence applies to skills as well as to objects. Our medieval ancestors cultivated and handed down, of necessity, numerous creative skills, making objects ranging from splendidly embossed armour to humble mutton-fat candles, none of which we any longer need. In more recent centuries a competent housewife had to be able to make her own furniture polish, or a soothing cream for bruises, or stitch the children's clothes, wants that are now supplied over the counter – or, increasingly, online.

The human ingenuity, talent and perseverance that once went into these necessary tasks is of course still with us, but today it is mainly devoted to such fields as medical research and to the ever-expanding world of digital communication. However, a few of the old skills that have largely disappeared are today cherished by select groups of people in the way that rare surviving actual objects are cherished. Making fine pottery in the traditional way is a much-favoured hobby and even full-time occupation. Thatching roofs, an art that fifty years ago seemed on the point

of extinction as old country thatchers died off, is now a flourishing and well-paid profession.

But many of the elements that each of us value most in our
individual lives cannot, realistically, be handed on. The particular
preoccupations of each life, and the rich, stored trivia of social
knowledge and emotional relationships, get largely consigned
to oblivion. The importance of memory as an aspect of being
human has long been recognised. In the pagan world of the
Norsemen, the chief god Odin was accompanied by two ravens,
one named 'Thought' and the other 'Memory'. Mnemosyne, the
goddess of memory, was one of the oldest in the Greek
pantheon. Yet in the ancient-Greek Underworld, once the dead
had been ferried by Charon across the river of Styx dividing
life from death, they came next to the waters of Lethe and
drank from this, after which many – though not all – earthly
memories disappeared. When Orpheus went intrepidly looking
for his departed Eurydice in the Underworld, allowed there by
the god of the Underworld only because of his inspired lyre-
playing, he found that Eurydice, though gentle and acquiescent
to his plans, had become shadowy and seemed only just to
remember him.

By the sheer going-on of time, we inexorably lose touch with
the dead; and it seems logical that the dead should also lose
touch with us. In past generations, when many Christians
believed without question that they would literally meet their
departed loved ones in Heaven – arriving, perhaps, in a joyful,
if decorous party where familiar faces would light up at their
approach – many must have had secret doubts about the feasi-
bility of this reunion. They must occasionally have wondered if,
after so many more years accumulated on Earth and so much

unshared experience, they would really find that much to say to a long-departed sister, mother or even child. And which of two genuinely beloved dead wives would greet the two-times widower? This problem, naïve as it may sound to present-day Christians, exercised some church-goers considerably in the nineteenth century. As Emily, the most intransigent of the Brontë sisters, wrote some years before her own death:

Cold in the earth – and fifteen wild Decembers
From these brown hills have melted into spring:
Faithful, indeed, is the spirit that remembers
After such years of change and suffering!

In an earlier paragraph I see that I have cited the classical myth of Orpheus and Eurydice as if I assume that all readers will be familiar with it. I realise, however, that this may not, today, be the case. Well-known stories from the Bible, which are more crucial than Greek gods to a general understanding of our culture, may not be readily recognised now, either. A massive depletion of the shared storehouse of popular memory has taken place, without those who should have been its guardians quite realising what was happening.

Fifty-odd years ago in Britain, when some form of daily religious Assembly and what was called Religious Education were standard in most schools, even children from non-believing families acquired a basic familiarity with Adam, Eve, Solomon, David, Moses, John the Baptist, the Nativity, the Good Samaritan, the wedding at Cana, the Last Supper, Judas Iscariot, Pontius Pilate, Mary Magdalene at the Tomb and often much more. Not everyone learnt a great deal about Graeco-Roman gods and

goddesses, but most did who made their way a little further up
the educational ladder, and so did those given a more expensive
education. For a number of reasons, this does not now happen.
It is as if 'all that junk' in the attic has been thrown out as
old-fashioned and 'irrelevant today', without anyone stopping
to examine the cultural value of what they were casting into
the skip.

This is a serious impoverishment of the popular memory and
a substantial impediment to the understanding of both art and
literature. The National Gallery today finds it necessary to run
courses to help willing but ignorant visitors decipher Christian
art, let alone art depicting the goings-on of more exotic deities.
University tutors in English complain that many students, even
though they have chosen Literature as their subject, find Milton's
Paradise Lost incomprehensible without a fundamental explanation as to what is meant by 'the Fall of man', a concept they
have not previously encountered.

The same collapse of general consensus as to what consti-
tutes a bedrock of cultural knowledge has also affected the
teaching of history. The brisk, old-fashioned trot (as in '1066
and All That') via who was a Good King and who a Bad one,
with a few side-steps into American Independence, the French
Revolution and Napoleon, till, aged about sixteen, one arrived
panting at somewhere approaching the twentieth century –
this trot may have been summary and limited and was
undoubtedly chauvinistic, but did provide a basic chronolog-
ical framework on which subsequent, more sophisticated study
could be hung. Today, the tendency both in school and at
university is, rather, to concentrate on specific topics, periods
or events, without necessarily relating them to a general

overview. Such study may be more detailed and globally aware than was the case in the past, but when it results (as it does) in a History graduate from a top university being unable to provide the date of the Battle of Waterloo, or even to say who fought the battle and in what circumstances, then something has gone wrong with our cultural transmission. Even an out-of-date and simplistic perception of such a landmark event (landmark not for the stir it made at the time, but for its far-reaching effects) is much more use than no knowledge at all.

It has been said that 'the past enters the present for reasons of the present'. Historical facts are constantly being reaccessed and reinterpreted to fit in with the preoccupations of each successive age. During the long period when power, conquest and authority were main preoccupations of the well-to-do classes, while first England and then Britain was establishing itself and seeing off European competitors, it was natural that 'History' was largely concerned with kings, conquerors, battles and conspiracies, as in Shakespeare's dramatised versions of past events. By and by, as the eighteenth century arrived and it became apparent that Britain might one day achieve her aim of being top nation, a strong leavening concept of Progress was added. The story that took over was the one generally, if misleadingly, known to us as 'the Whig view of history'. In this version (still widely adhered to today) it is in the natural order of things for 'civilisation' gradually to triumph over 'barbarism'. History, when recounted, needs a plot, including myths of cause, effect and intention. So we are all, it is assumed, on a journey – even if with setbacks – from metaphorical darkness into light: *'Lighten our darkness, we beseech*

Thee, O Lord, and by thy great mercy defend us from all perils and dangers ... '

It seems clear that the overview of history has been much influenced by biblical myths. The Bible, especially the Old Testament, is after all the mythic narrative of the creation of a people, with special emphasis on an escape from slavery into freedom. The themes of Fall and Salvation are similarly present in many modern historical accounts. Other biblical events have provided encouraging stereotypes with which later events may be compared, especially the David-slaying-Goliath story, which has been evoked each time an apparently smaller British force has seen off a powerful alien one – as in the Battles of the Armada, Trafalgar and the 1940 Battle of Britain. Determined individual leaders such as Francis Drake, Horatio Nelson and, indeed, Robin Hood, who may or may not actually have existed, have been readily placed in the David role. In other Christian cultures the occasional individual, from Hitler to Che Guevara, has been promoted as if he were a supra-normal being, possibly even a Christ-figure, not quite like others.

But each era has its own preoccupations, which the perception of the past is revised to fit. The past as recounted from the Latin of the Bible by medieval monks, who were usually the only literate people in their world, was rather different from that of the upper classes of the eighteenth century. The education of this latter sort consisted almost entirely of the literature of the Greeks and Romans. Somewhat naturally, they took their uplifting models and their version of history from this ancient world, ignoring all the centuries that had intervened, and so construed their present in those terms also. As Karl Marx noted, 'The French Revolution was enacted in Roman dress.' Judging from the number of eighteenth- and early-nineteenth-century figures whose memorial statues stand around in our cities today wearing togas, a good many other events of national significance took place mentally in the classical world, including a number of small European wars.

Today, very few people have much familiarity with Latin, let alone Greek, and our preoccupations lie elsewhere. It has been said that too much of our current perception of past eras is about empathy – about yearning indignantly over the misfortunes and ill-treatments suffered by other people in other times, often with the added complaint that history itself is at fault because it has not given proper prominence to these nameless participants. Kings, statesmen and battles are dismissed as irrelevant, and concentration is on the poor, the ordinary, the working classes, the exploited, the huddled masses. Even the anchoring of historical events to dates may be stigmatised as 'dry as dust', as if knowing that something took place in 1536 or 1789 somehow prevented one from feeling adequate modern moral outrage at the plight of silk-workers, Highlanders, black people, women or whichever group is being posthumously championed. The remote descendants of their oppressors may be required to express shame and apology on behalf of their ancestors.

Some academics, exasperated by the myopia of this approach, have been inclined to blame twentieth-century left-wing historians for it, but the most famous of them, the Marxist E.P. Thompson, himself spoke out in his *The Making of the English Working Class* against 'the enormous condescension of posterity'. Essentially, we cannot claim to espouse fully the realities of those who went before us because there is no way we can share their vantage-point or their assumptions. We know what happened subsequently. They couldn't know. We also need to bear in mind that, just because we know their future, that does not mean it was inevitable. Things could have turned out otherwise. The admirably sane twentieth-century French philosopher Raymond Aron (who eschewed the absolutist formulations of his contemporaries) claimed that 'we should put back into the past the same level of uncertainty that we feel in the present'. There is a tendency for people in every single era to feel especially afflicted by change, that they – today we – are moving on some unprecedented and dangerous frontier of time, going we-know-not-where. The truth is that every generation before us has felt the same way, with the same uninformed apprehension about the unknowable years to come.

It has been suggested that the decline in the stock of general knowledge relating to both history and myth has created an unnamed public need for something to replace these traditional sources, and that the result has been a newly reborn taste for complex but moral fantasy tales. This was first noticed in the 1960s with the extraordinary popularity, even among young adults, of C.S. Lewis's *Chronicles of Narnia*, and it seems confirmed today by the huge success of J.K. Rowling's *Harry Potter* books and, indeed, those of the determinedly unbelieving Philip Pullman. By the same token, historical novels over the last generation have emerged from the romantic-fiction category into something more demanding, literary and intricately researched. Hilary Mantel's tour de force in her re-creation of Tudor England comes to mind – but so does C.J. Sansom's energetic and detailed evocation of the same era in true-crime-detection formula. However estranged we have become from what, for many generations, was our folk memory, we want to *know* about the past. We want to *feel* it.

Television series, both good and bad, about life long ago are popular, including those that involve real present-day people, who are not actors, dressing and living for a short while as if actually in 'a Victorian slum' or 'an Edwardian family home'. Huge audiences have basked for several years with borrowed nostalgia in such series as *Upstairs, Downstairs* and *Downton Abbey*, while visiting actual country houses, nicely decked out as if most of the twentieth century had never happened, has become a mass summer-weekend occupation. A video-game[32] involving a chase through an intricate vista of London in 1868 has a nonsensical central plot, but its setting is scrupulously derived from genuine sources and has had wide appeal. It is often – and probably truthfully – been said that the digital world, with all its spurious excitements, is a destroyer of cultural heritage and shared memory. However, digital technology can bring vanished places to life for us as never before. A charming but static print of, say, the City of London in Dickens's time, or New York when fields began at Harlem, can today be transformed into a motion picture of that very scene.

I do not think, though, that the present-day passion for retrieving something of the lost past is really due to the gift of modern technology, helpful though that may be. Some other need is at work. It is as if we want to bridge gaps in time in the same way that, with jet travel and Skype, we bridge space. We want to 'get in touch' with our ancestors through records that are now accessible on the Internet, even if we cannot do so in quite the same way that we get in touch with family or friends on the other side of the world. Long ago, if a brother or son went to America, Australia or only as far as India, places that sailing ships took months to reach or to return from, you were unlikely to retain much meaningful contact. It was almost as if he had died. 'We never expect to live to be blessed with a sight of you,' a father wrote from Scotland[33] to his young son in Bombay around 1790, 'but while we have agreeable accounts of your health and happiness we ought to bless God and be satisfied.' Today, we expect to retain some degree of ongoing relationship, even apparently with the dead.

In 2018, a four-year commemoration of the First World War on film, television and radio, and by intermittent live ceremonies, finally drew to its close. Old film was remastered and rerun, recordings made when old soldiers were still alive were brought out of the archive and copiously broadcast. Poppies were displayed in enormous and beautiful profusion, present-day members of the royal family stood to attention in Flanders alongside both French and German notables, evoking their shared dead. On 1st July 2016 commuters on their usual journey to work, arriving at main stations in London and several other cities, were surprised and then touched to find at each one a crowd of young men in the army uniforms of the '14–'18 standing motionless. If approached and spoken to, none of the men would reply. Each would simply hand a card to the person who had approached him, a card which explained that they were men who had gone out to fight on the first, murderous day of the Battle of the Somme and never returned, and which individual name he represented. The dead cannot, of course, speak.

How different is this passionate and persistent contact with the past from the general habit in earlier generations! It so happened that during the First World War the centenary came round of the notable, final battle of the Napoleonic War, the encounter at Waterloo in June 1815. The British only just won, probably because allied Prussian reinforcements turned up in time. Wellington himself, in command of the allied troops, admitted at the time that it had been 'a damned close-run thing'. It was in the end an undoubted victory, with Napoleon taken prisoner for ever, but the numbers of men on both sides who were killed or died afterwards from their injuries are estimated to have approached fifty thousand. A good third of them would have been British, with another ten thousand perhaps from their Flemish and Prussian allies. Waterloo is regarded as having been the single most concentrated loss of human life ever recorded in one day's battle, worse even than the notorious first day of the Battle of the Somme a hundred and one years later.

Did the dead of Waterloo then, in 1915, benefit from some brief but heartfelt ceremony evoking their memory and their sacrifice? No, they did not. Of course the British were otherwise engaged, fighting off (this time) the Germans, with the French as friends – but even had they not been so preoccupied, it is hard to imagine that much commemoration would have gone on. For between 1815 and 1915 lay a vast gulf of technological, social and visible change, far greater than that which separates us today from 1915. In 1915 London was already huge, seamed with bus routes and underground lines, with motor cars multiplying in the streets, cinemas opening, telephones and typewriters in every office, police stations, post offices, any number of newspapers, public lavatories – the whole panoply of a great city essentially as it still is today. There was already a network of free hospitals. Schools, too, had been built everywhere, free and obligatory. There were street hawkers and poverty, but old-age pensions were paid, as were lifetime pensions to the widows of the men dying in France. If we entered that London, we would basically feel at home in it.

In 1815 London did not stretch even to the present-day inner suburbs. The site of the Elephant and Castle was swampy fields. There were tile kilns and a vast midden[34] where the great stations would later rise on the Euston Road. There were no stations; railway trains had not been invented, and a steam-boat service on the Thames for short trips was only just beginning. There were not even horse-buses as yet, either. No proper drainage system. No police. Few schools and most of them not free. No cheap or rapid postal service, no cheap newspapers. Very few social safety-nets for the poor, and those that existed were out-of-date and inadequate. Very little regard for the needs of individuals, who lived and died as best they could, just as every generation had before them. All this is the other side to the beguiling rurality we see in many late-Georgian views of London and whose loss we now lament. Understandably, the man or woman of a hundred years later, the product of many decades of Victorian industrial prosperity, urban expansion and pride, would feel remote from this antique world of the past and thus from the great-grandfather who had died at Waterloo – if they even knew that such had been their ancestor's fate.

There, too, a huge change had set in. Through the harrowing years of the war of 1914–18 names of those dying at the front were continuously noted, bodies were collected on the field, when they could be, and hastily buried with prayers in temporary graves. After the war, all these remains – or all that could still be located, after the land had been battered and pulverised for four years – were moved with extraordinary labour and care to great, quiet orderly cemeteries with line after line of stones both named and nameless. At the same time the hundreds and thousands of dead soldiers of whom no identifiable trace had been found were recorded on huge memorials: 'Their name liveth for evermore.'

In 1815, however, all but the notably rich and grand, from both sides of the battle, were flung into common pits, along with the dead horses. The official system for sending word of ordinary soldiers' deaths back to their families was haphazard and inadequate. So it had always been, throughout history. In quiet English cemeteries, too, as in continental ones, the great mass of people, before the nineteenth century, had no permanent and marked graves.

The red corn-poppy, so familiar to us now from countless memorial wreaths, was not made a symbol of lasting commemoration till the First World War, when it figured in the poem 'In Flanders fields the poppies blow ...' by a poet of that war[35] who is now famed mainly for the enduring image he contributed. Yet, in previous eras, poppies had been associated rather with forgetting, on account of that species of poppy, which is the raw material of opium. In the seventeenth century the writer, philosopher and alchemist Sir Thomas Browne could write: 'The iniquity of oblivion blindly scattereth her poppy, and deals with the memory of men without distinction to merit of perpetuity.'

No longer. It is as if, at some point in the nineteenth century, along with so much material and social change and transformation of habitat, a point was reached at which the nature and persistence of memory itself began to change, and grow.

CHAPTER XIV

False History and Favourite Myths

Time, as experienced, notoriously speeds up or slows down according to the events it contains. A time of rapid change, social or physical, has the effect of making the relatively recent past seem more distant than it really is. There have been other periods of our history, well before the nineteenth century with its symbolic railway trains cutting across the landscape of life, when people clearly felt that time had speeded up, leaving their remembered early years behind in some quaint Other Place.

One of these times in England was the Civil War of the mid-seventeenth century, when in the space of less than a decade the king went from being in that position by Divine Right, supposedly capable of curing various diseases simply by his touch, to a felon tried and beheaded for treason. As a contemporary observer of these changes wrote: 'The old world is running up like paper in the fire.' The rule by the parliamentary party, under Cromwell, that set in towards the end of the 1640s was in intention moralistic and authoritarian, but in practice the Civil War had destabilised society and crime was rife. Youths who had enlisted on Cromwell's side, perhaps seduced by the heady notion of a more equal society or simply in the hope of a good fight, found themselves turned loose on their own resources. Trade, both at home and with neighbouring countries, had suffered while men were otherwise busying themselves. The care of London's fabric, including the all-important water-conduits, had been neglected. Many members of the old ruling class were dead, or impoverished, or had taken refuge abroad like Ralph Verney, or quarrelled bitterly with each other for having supported the opposing side. In practice, this shake-up of society had the long-term positive effect of driving the surviving sons of landed families into lucrative commerce, particularly with distant lands such as the Levant, Persia, India and the New World. But in the shorter term it made educated, thoughtful men like the diarist John Evelyn, who returned from discreet exile in France in 1652, feel that there had been a profound change for the worse.

Some fifteen years later, when royalty had once again been restored and the Cromwellian 'Interregnum' itself was beginning to seem like a remote bad dream, Evelyn's wife Mary wrote in her diary, ' … what we read of the dead seems a fable, so different is the present practice of the world'.

Mary was sixteen years younger than her husband (Evelyn had been born before Charles I even came to the throne), but her childhood had begun in Royalist times: her father became ambassador in Paris, which is where the family were sheltered from the worst of the Civil War and where Evelyn met her. Both of them, as it turned out, lived on through the successive power-shifts that followed the Restoration of 1660 and into the following century. By then, in the circles in which the Evelyns moved, what was called New Learning, both scientific and philosophical, was much to the fore. Constitutional monarchy of a kind recognisable today was beginning to take shape. Witchcraft was officially declared to be a delusion for silly old women. The practice of hanging, drawing, quartering – or simply burning – individuals because they professed the wrong religion had been left behind in the unregretted past. Yet this was also the first era in which 'the shipwreck of history' began to be investigated and studied in a way resembling a modern historical approach. Antiquarianism too had become fashionable, and though some people regarded it as an obsession with old stones devoid of a moral message, others understood its potential better. Old stones, especially those threatened with destruction, became the energetic and painstaking preoccupation of some very intelligent people, who wished to map out the route by which their civilisation had arrived at its present state. Intellectually, the days of Queen Anne, with the Hanoverians waiting in the wings to take over, were a world away from brutal early-Stuart times.

And yet – the fabled dead of a hundred-plus years before, who seemed to Mary Evelyn to belong to some old story, had themselves seen a remarkable shipwreck of a familiar world and the construction of a new one. Between 1529, when Henry VIII declared that he, rather than the Pope, was head of the Church in England, and 1558, when Queen Elizabeth I came to the throne and some relative degree of order was restored, or rather remade, the social fabric of Britain was rent from top to bottom. Not only were queens, bishops and what we would now recognise as high-ranking civil servants put to death in succession under Henry, but his teenage son Edward VI, indoctrinated by his advisers, encouraged the Reformation still further. With the destruction of the monasteries and the dispersal of the monks and clerics to death, destitution or a discreet adoption of the new faith (according to taste and luck), a major part of the structure of everyday life was destroyed. Who would now keep the records, run great land-holdings with worldly wisdom and prudence – and who would look after and shelter the poor, the afflicted, the inconvenient or the merely rather odd? Religious houses had provided homes and occupations, of a sort, for people of all kinds, from the richest to the poorest. Yet now they stood derelict and vandalised. A whole, informal, patchy but often effective social-service system had been abruptly dismantled.

> Bitter, bitter, O, to behold
> The grass to grow
> Where the walls of Walsingham
> So stately did show ...
>
> ... Owls do shriek where the sweetest hymns
> Lately were sung;
> Toads and serpents hold their dens
> Where the palmers did throng.

The manuscript from which this comes (today in the Bodleian Library, Oxford) is believed to have been written during his long imprisonment by the staunchly and traditionally Catholic Earl of Arundel. But it was not only those who adhered to the practices of the old faith who mourned the changes, any more than it was only the physical dissolution of the religious houses, chantries and shrines that affected the more pragmatic and pliable general population. The Reformation, in the form in which it finally settled down under Elizabeth, also did away with many of the traditional church festivals – Candlemas, Lammastide, Michaelmas and so on – and with the ancient and riotous street-plays that had accompanied them. Purgatory, too, was declared a non-place, an unworthy illusion. For ordinary parishioners it was 'a stripping away of familiar and beloved observances, the destruction of a vast and resonant world of symbols which ... they both understood and controlled'.[36]

And of course a further layer of uncertainty was added by the fact that, after Edward's young death in 1553 and the nine-day debacle that ended in another potential young monarch losing her head (Lady Jane Grey), Mary became queen and did her best to restore Roman Catholicism as the one true faith. It was the turn of the prominent Protestant clerics now to face execution. The ordinary people did not know where they were – and knew still less when, five years later, Mary died in turn and it was her half-sister Elizabeth who was installed on the throne. Surviving Wills of the time sometimes confidently leave money to supposedly restored monasteries, or for Masses to be said for the testator's soul, as if these reinstated things were now going to remain a permanent part of the shifting religious scene. However, more cautious testators tended to add to such behests extra clauses on the lines of 'if the laws of the realm will permit this'. In fact the Act of Uniformity the following year did not permit: it abolished the Mass, reintroduced a prayer book in English and set the country definitively on the route to what eventually became the Protestant Anglican Church.

No wonder the further round of low-church fervour the following century, with more destruction under Cromwell of crosses, angels, wall-paintings, stained glass and even the attempted abolition of Christmas, left most of the population by the second half of the seventeenth century in favour simply of a little peace and toleration.

One result of all this change, which (as Mary Evelyn remarked) made the activities of earlier generations 'seem like a fable', was that overtly partisan history was finally abandoned. Kings were no longer divine (though Queen Anne had a wistful hope in that direction); the present no longer had to be justified by retelling the past to fit it. It is clear from the plays of Shakespeare and his contemporaries, two or three generations earlier, that that was very much what they had been doing. The Tudors, and hence the Stuarts, had to be justified as the rightful, God-given monarchs. As a result, the image that we have all inherited of Henry V as a splendid and honourable leader, taken from Shakespeare's play of that name and enhanced by more than one twentieth-century film version of his text, has diverged far from the brutal reality of his times in a way that now seems uncorrectable. Similarly, the image of Richard III, the last Plantagenet king, who died in battle at Bosworth and whose grave in Leicester was little regarded and then lost for the next five hundred years, is almost immovably fixed in popular history as the evil cripple who murdered his nephews, the Little Princes in the Tower. Since his fortunate rediscovery beneath a council car park, efforts have been made to rehabilitate his memory and to insist that the villain of the time was actually the future Tudor king Henry VII, but since the truth is now almost certainly irrecoverable, it seems doubtful if his image can ever be entirely redrawn.

In fact the princes themselves are a classic example of what may be false history gaining an unshakable moral hold on the popular imagination. It is known that when their father, Edward IV, died, the elder of the princes was declared to be Edward V. He was only twelve, so his Uncle Richard stood Regent for him. He was accommodated in the Tower of London (then still a palace rather than a prison). The mother of the boys, Elizabeth Woodville, thinking that her son would be bored and lonely without a playmate, asked that his younger brother might join him, and this was granted. These are known facts. It is also reported that, for the first weeks they were together, the boys were to be seen practising on a green lawn within the Tower with their bows and arrows, just as present-day brothers would be seen taking football shots together at a makeshift goal.

However, after a while they were seen no more. They were never seen again. Later that same year Richard had himself crowned king, on the grounds that Elizabeth Woodville had been married to someone else before marrying Edward IV and so the princes were illegitimate. But this did not, apparently, create the public furore that you might expect.

What was going on? Did people simply believe that Richard might be right, that a child-king was a bad idea anyway, and that the princes had probably just been spirited away to France? Did anyone actually ask? It was known, in any case, that the boy-king had been in poor health and that he thought, for this or another reason, that he might soon die: he frequently requested the comfort of priestly absolution. Yet there does appear to have been a widespread belief to the effect that the boys remained alive, since, in the following decade, not one but two pretenders to the throne were produced, the memorably named Lambert Simnel and Perkin Warbeck. Simnel claimed to be Edward V himself, while Warbeck, a few years later, was presented as the younger prince. Neither seems to have been especially convincing, though each had their supporters. Richard III was dead by now, Henry VII was on the throne, and clearly he was not going to let himself be dislodged.

The whole story then appears to have gone quiet while the rest of the Tudor dynasty unrolled and Shakespeare's plays had their effect. Not till a hundred and ninety years after the boys had last been seen, in the utterly different times of Charles II and the New Learning, did building works on a staircase near the White Tower reveal two skeletons, which were declared to be those of two young males. King Charles II himself accepted that these were probably the lost 'Princes in the Tower' and thus the story was further consolidated. The bones were reburied in Westminster Abbey in an urn designed by Sir Christopher Wren – though as several years elapsed between their discovery and their reinterment, it is not quite sure that what was reburied was entirely the right set of bones.

Over the following two or three centuries theories tending to rehabilitate Richard intermittently appeared, including the suggestion that the villain of the piece may have been, not Uncle Richard, but distant cousin Henry VII. The urn was finally reopened and its contents rather perfunctorily re-examined in the 1930s, in line with the scientific limitations of the time. It was remarked then that it was not even clear that both skeletons were male.

The rediscovery of Richard's remains in 2012, the retrieval of his own DNA and that of his distant descendants has led to fervent demands from some quarters that the Princes' urn should be opened again. It has been suggested that modern analysis of the bones might well show there is no family link with Richard, as there should be, if those are indeed his young nephews lying there. However, this request has been firmly rejected by the Church, the Crown and those directly in charge of Westminster Abbey.[37] It is pointed out that it is not the business of the Church to hunt down ancient deceptions or errors in hallowed ground. If the bones were to turn out to have nothing to do with the Princes, no one would know what to do with them, or with their grand urn – or with the unverified contents of a number of other ancient coffins and caskets beneath the abbey floors, should further truth-revealing exhumations be demanded. And that even if the bones were found to be genuine, no amount of sophisticated DNA analysis could reveal just when the boys died and by whose hand.

But it makes no difference. The image of the doomed young-sters, boys just like our own, huddled together in one bed as their closet-assassins approach one summer night in 1483, is so powerful an indictment of the evil of the past – and thus, by contrast, proof of the progress that we have made over the centuries, in spite of all – that we are unlikely to discard the Little Princes in the Tower anytime soon.

Perhaps the best example of a false history in our Western tra-dition, and certainly one of the grandest, is the well-known Arthurian legend, with all its ramifications into image-enhancing Romance and national myths of origin. Did King Arthur ever actually exist?

There is no final answer to the question. It has been reason-ably suggested that, as the Romans were withdrawing from

Britain circa AD 400 there may well have been an Arthur-like leader figure, or several, in different parts of Britain, around whom some form of independence movement coalesced. If so, such a person was very likely to have been of mixed Romano-Celtic heritage, a product in himself of the Roman occupation. Alternatively, it has been suggested that the Arthurian figure or figures date from slightly later, when, in the wake of the Roman departure, the Angles and Saxons were invading from the nearest point of the European mainland, and that the resistance was against these newcomers who were indeed driving the indigenous Celtic people into the remoter parts of the British Isles. What is known is that the earliest reports of an Arthur-figure do seem to have been taken to France by the Welsh, via Celtic Brittany, in the fifth and sixth centuries.

The story then vegetates there for some hundreds of years, till it begins to return to Britain in the wake of the Norman invasions, which created there a new Franco-British upper class. Its first imaginative recounting, to promote the concept of knightly chivalry, is usually ascribed to the late-twelfth-century French poet and courtier Chrétien de Troyes: the unlikely character of the noble Lancelot, the 'very perfect gentle knight', first makes his appearance in de Troyes's work. But Arthur also figures towards the middle of that century in the work in Britain of an Augustinian monk. This energetic man, Geoffrey of Monmouth, busied himself with an *Historia Regum Britanniae*, History of the Kingdom of Britain. The very title proclaims a desire to gather up assorted stories into one coherent myth of origin. Monmouth included, in this and in his other writings, a good deal of genuine history of local kings, but his essential aim was to trace the genesis of Britain back to the mythical Brutus of Troy.

This person (who does not actually seem to have existed in any form, though at least one professional genealogist[38] has tried hard to find some substance for his story) was allegedly descended from Aeneas, who was himself the product of an encounter between a god and a mortal (see and compare Jesus Christ). He was said to have led the enslaved Trojans from slavery into freedom (see Moses), eventually bringing them to 'Albion' (Britain), where they sailed up the River Dart and landed close to present-day Totnes, in Devon. This Brutus slew two giants called Gog and Magog, founded Oxford and London, sired King Arthur (a neat connection there) and hence a long line of rightful kings.

The Celtic elements, especially the giants and the Arthurian legend, seem to have been added to the Brutus legend by Monmouth. He may have been responsible also for the founder-of-London myth, although the fantasies now attached to the still-existing 'London stone', which is probably a piece of surviving Roman masonry reused as a medieval waymark, were not all his responsibility, but a later addition. Nor was he the inventor of the 'King-Arthur-will-return', *rex quondam rexque futurus*, re-creation of the Jerusalem myth. In subsequent centuries this myth attached itself to the Arthurian story as part of a theme of sin and redemption – see once more the Jesus Christ parallels. As a twentieth-century director of the British Museum[39] put it: 'extraneous oddments ... in the course of the Middle Ages stuck themselves like burrs to the accommodating body of [Monmouth's] History'. The Tudors, too, when they came along, had a vested interest in emphasising, through their descent from Owen Tudor, their ancient British origins.

The Arthurian strand was also given a boost in the late fifteenth century by the appearance of Sir Thomas Malory's *Le Morte d'Arthur*, compiled in English from various existing French sources, probably by the Thomas Malory who was a semi-criminal landowner and participant in the Wars of the Roses. He had time to write during several long spells in prison. It is he who seems to have introduced the concept of the search for the 'holy grail', which has proved such a fruitful source of invention for much more recent writers. Malory gave his book an English name: its French title was given it by Caxton, who printed it. In print, the book reached many more readers than any manuscript could have done in the still-recent pre-printing days. The Arthurian legend was beginning to be a staple of the English view of their own history.

But so was the related, interwoven Brutus legend, and in the following century both Spenser and Milton incorporated this into their major works. It disappeared after the Restoration, when myths of Roman origins were preferred, but surfaced again in the course of the eighteenth century. Towards the end of that century came William Blake, with his visionary view of London itself as a 'new Jerusalem', giving a further philosophic dimension to the whole parcel of dreams. In the nineteenth century the Arthurian element came graphically to the fore again with a newly discovered artistic and literary preoccupation with all things medieval. Today, the Arthurian and Brutus myths, encouraged by the ease of modern travel from one 'sacred site' to another, and augmented by assorted references to Druids, 'white witches', 'the old faith', paganism, and with some Irish, transatlantic or

Israeli lost tribes added in, is still developing. Clearly, there is a perceived need for it.

Compared with the huge and still-burgeoning extent of the Arthur–Brutus mythology, most examples of false history are quite small and self-contained. There is, for instance, the well-known desire to associate any very old building with some easily identifiable celebrity, hence no doubt the insistence in ancient houses up and down the country that 'Queen Elizabeth I slept here' – though it is true that the lady did travel around her kingdom a good deal. There is also a marked tendency to associate the 'gentleman of the highway', Dick Turpin, with surviving medieval houses that have no verifiable connection with the violent and sadistic eighteenth-century criminal that Turpin actually was. His speciality was attacking isolated Essex farmhouses along with other gang members, and threatening and torturing the inhabitants into parting with any wealth they had. Why the swaggering, supposedly courtly highwayman has become a popular English myth, a kind unknown, I believe, in other European countries, is a mystery in its own right.

Other fantasy stories tend to arise out of a need to reinforce a currently fashionable preoccupation. For example, much has been made recently of a supposed hitherto-unnoticed 'diversity' in sixteenth- and seventeenth-century London, with occasional baptism or burial records that record 'an heathen' or 'a blackamoor' pulled out of context and exhibited as if they were examples of many more. The truth is, rather, that while a very few people of noticeably dark skin, mainly Berbers from North Africa, arrived one way or another in Britain in the early modern period (including an envoy from Morocco who is thought to have been the model for Shakespeare's Othello[40]), the actual numbers were very small. Which is why such people stood out.

To misinterpret historical records, through ignorance or, worse, sentimentality, does no favour to the group being discussed. A particularly egregious example occurred in a short television documentary about City burial grounds, which was shown in 2016. The amiable but ill-chosen young presenter speculated hopefully that the fairly frequent presence in burial records of the term 'a stranger' might indicate that London then had many people from far-off places, and that the term might indicate darkness of skin and hence the presence of a whole population of hitherto-unrecognised 'slaves' ... In fact, as any amateur historian could have told him and as the researchers for the programme certainly should have told him, 'stranger' was simply the term used for centuries in such records for the burial of anyone not actually registered as dwelling in that parish – a father, say, who had died while being cared for in the house of his son, or a daughter who had returned to her mother in the neighbouring village for a childbirth that then ended sadly.

The most flagrant modern example of someone supposedly black-skinned being elevated to a symbolic role they themselves would certainly have rejected in life is Mary Seacole, now treated as an informal patron saint of all nurses from the Caribbean. A statue has been erected to her in the courtyard of St Thomas' Hospital, London, and it is claimed that she was born into slave society and combated 'prejudice', including that of Florence Nightingale, in order to nurse wounded Crimean soldiers. But in reality Mrs Seacole, although no doubt skilled at generally caring for people, was not a nurse and did not try to be one. Aged then about fifty, she was what was called by the army a 'suttler', a provider of food and other necessities or desires, and was undoubtedly an efficient businesswoman and social climber. She ran a 'hotel' in the Crimea – more properly a canteen – that was popular with officers recovering from minor wounds or illnesses. Born in 1805, she was the daughter not of a slave, but of a mixed-race boarding-house keeper in Jamaica and a Scottish soldier. In other words, she was from a group then known as 'mulatto', or 'créole', which was then acceptable in all but the most exclusive circles of British society. There were mixed-race officers in the British army, and most distinguished British families with long-term Indian connections were admitted to have some dark blood. Lord Liverpool, who was Prime Minister for a very long term in the early nineteenth century, was known to have had an Indian grandmother. Mrs Seacole stated in her autobiography,[41] 'I am only a little brown' (a fact that photos of her bear out), and she would certainly have been shocked and annoyed to be classed today as black, since she and her kind looked down upon blacks.

I am not the first person to point these facts out. The argument about whether it can ever be excusable, let alone desirable, to perpetrate a false view of history in the aim of some supposed public good is a long-lasting one. Perhaps it is best to consign the real Mary Seacole to the pages of genuine history books and to regard the newly resurrected public figure of her as something akin to King Arthur of myth: a useful fable.

Often, of course, a fantasy view is perpetrated by people who badly want it to be true. For every successful imposter, whether a Lambert Simnel or an 'Anastasia' claiming to be a daughter of the last Tsar of Russia and to have survived the execution of the family at Yekaterinburg in 1918, there has to be a person, or people, who feel a passionate need to believe the story they are being told.

The Tsar's two sisters escaped from the Russian Revolution to Germany, also the country of their dead sister-in-law, the last Tsarina. In the early 1920s a woman calling herself 'Anna', who had apparently been rescued from a suicide attempt in the River Spree at Berlin, was presented to the sisters. She claimed to be the youngest daughter of the Romanov family and to have been protected from the assassins' bullets in the Yekaterinburg cellar by the jewels stitched into her bodice. The story was not very likely: the family had been subjected to knife attacks as well as multiple bullets, and the mere fact that the remains of one of the princesses had not, then, been located was not a strong argument. However the Grand Duchesses were aunts to the murdered Romanov children. They had lost all their closest relatives, their home, their country, their wealth and their status: it was understandable that one of them, at any rate, looked for a while as if she was going to accept 'Anna' as her lost niece.

But the fact that the girl could not apparently speak or understand Russian eventually gave even the yearning duchess pause for thought. It presently became apparent that 'Anna' was probably a mentally deranged Polish factory worker called Franziska Schanzkowska, and as, over the years, other false Anastasias appeared here and there in central Europe, even the most homesick and credulous of the one-time Russian elite became sceptical. Many decades later, with the discovery of more buried remains, modern DNA tests proved that whoever 'Anna' was, she was nothing to do with the Romanovs. But her story still surfaces at regular intervals today, in the popular press and even in serious Eastern European historical publications.

*

Such imposters – some of whom may believe their own stories – are the walking embodiment of a very well-known poem by the Russian Second World War poet Konstantin Simonov, which begins *'Wait for me and I will return, only wait very hard.'*

After a saga of dreary seasons of snow and heat succeeding one another, when news never comes, nor any letter – *'Wait even when you are told you should forget./ Wait even when my mother and son think I am no more,* – the lost one at long last returns: *'So I came back. Because you went on waiting for me when no one else did.'*

I have heard the poem described as 'emotionally lethal', since it gives validity to the vainest of false hopes: that of feeling that one's own conviction just may be enough to keep the lost person alive, and that simply by abandoning hope one may therefore be consigning that person to death and oblivion.

This belief is not uncommon in wartime, and surfaced particularly strongly towards the end of the First World War, on account of the number of missing men whose bodies would never be recovered. Here and there, in the years immediately after that war, imposters surfaced, men hoping perhaps to extract money from a well-to-do family who had lost an only son, claiming typically to be a wartime friend of the son, with an elaborately fabricated reason as to why funds must be sent abroad to 'rescue' him. Some families, in their grief, were all too ready to fall victim to this fraud. And other ex-soldiers, lost souls who either through head-injury or psychological trauma had no clear perception themselves of who they were, became sucked helplessly into family daydreams based on mistaken identity.

The best-documented and most long-drawn-out of these cases occurred in France, with a Frenchman who became known as 'the Living Unknown Soldier' – by analogy with the dead ones who would soon be laid symbolically in Westminster Abbey, under the Arc de Triomphe in Paris, in Arlington Cemetery in Washington DC, in Moscow and in several other locations. In February 1918, in the last year of the war, a trainload of French prisoners-of-war who were wounded or otherwise disabled was sent back from Germany to France. One was found wandering on Lyons station, apparently amnesiac: he had no identity paper or tag, but eventually seemed to give his name as Anselme, or Adrien, Mangin. No such person appeared in the army lists and, as he was clearly not in a fit state to be left to his own devices, he was sent to an asylum.

There followed well over ten years of fruitless efforts on the part of several different doctors on the one hand, and several different families on the other, to establish who 'Mangin' really was and to whom he might therefore be said to belong. Amazing as it may seem, although the sufferer showed no signs of recognising anyone and seemed to have no desire to, he was firmly claimed as their own by several sets of people whose own local accents were quite different from his vaguely Parisian-region enunciation. One widow in particular was so insistent that, although the superintendent of the asylum did not really believe her, he was very much inclined to let her take Mangin home with her as some sort of solution for all concerned: 'Like many before her, Madame Lemay, totally convinced of having found her husband in Mangin, is apt to retain from what she sees or hears only what will support her position.'

This bizarre story did not, however, have a happy ending. Even as Madame Lemay was winning her case against three other vociferous claimants, yet another family at last emerged. Their name was Monjoin, and they were not actually looking for their brother Octave, whom they believed to have been killed in the war. They merely wanted to get a proper death-certificate to settle a family dispute over a Will. Assorted lawsuits continued; it was not till the late 1930s that the Monjoin identification was finally decided by a court, and even then Madame Lemay once more appealed against it. By 1940, when Germany invaded France for the second time in the century, the Living Unknown Soldier was still isolated in an asylum, unwanted by those who had the only legal claim on him. Under the Occupation, few French people had energy to spare for the useless and pathetic, and the Germans, with their programme of eugenics, had still less. Mangin-Monjoin died of sepsis from an old wound in a Parisian hospital in November 1942.[42]

The identification even of the genuinely dead of that war has posed problems also. Over the decades, farming or development in the Flanders–Pas de Calais area or the Ardennes has occasionally brought to light small collections of bodies, buried hastily in ad hoc graves near where they fell, and overlooked by the post-war body-retrieval squads. When, in 1991, a body that seemed to be that of the French writer Alain Fournier was found with others in a small wood, various circumstances suggested that the death of this young hero as early as September 1914 had not been as glorious as readers of his one great novel, Le Grand Meaulnes, would have wished. It rather looked, indeed, as if he and another officer had found a posse of Germans and had shot them all out of hand at close range, before being killed themselves. The whole lot had been buried in a mass grave by the German forces. The emotion this engendered in French literary circles has not died down to this day.

An odder saga of identification occurred with Rudyard Kipling's only son, John. And this one bizarrely touches my own family – once again, the Jacobs.

As many readers will know, John Kipling was killed in 1915, and Rudyard Kipling never forgave himself for urging his boy to join up in the first place. John was a gentle person, severely short-sighted, and when the war broke out he was only seventeen. He was not one of those young men longing to go off to fight, declaring, 'Now, God be thanked, Who has matched us with His hour'[43] and fearing that if they did not hurry the war would be 'over by Christmas'. With an eagerness that shocks today, and was a great source of remorse to Kipling in the long years after the war, the father approached his influential friends in government to get this under-age recruit inserted into some illustrious regiment. He was politely rebuffed – but eventually he managed to get John a commission in the Irish Guards. There was no family connection with Ireland, but possibly those in charge were more relaxed than their English counterparts and were also flattered by the idea of having the son of the famous Kipling in the regiment.

John went off, with the glasses without which he was blind held on by tape, to be trained in marksmanship. Immediately after his eighteenth birthday the boy was sent to France as a second lieutenant in command of men. The Battle of Loos of autumn 1915 became a slaughter. On 27th September Second

Lieutenant Kipling was last seen, wounded in the face, by his sergeant, who hesitated to approach because he saw that the boy-officer was crying and might not want to be noticed by an NCO in that state.

His body was apparently located many days later by an army padre, who reported that he had interred it, along with others, with a hasty prayer. By the end of the war, after endless back-and-forth fighting and shelling over that ground, the remains were, like so many others, irrecoverable.

Rudyard and Carrie Kipling did not receive the padre's account till much later, and appeared to believe it might be a case of mistaken identity anyway. Having had one of the fatal telegrams telling them their son was 'missing', they launched into a campaign of search for him, enlisting the support of numerous influential acquaintances, refusing – like many others – to accept that their son was simply dead. Their fruitless enquiries and hypotheses continued for years, even after the war was ended and the unidentifiable remains of thousands upon thousands of men were being disinterred and moved into permanent cemeteries. The standard phrase to be placed on each grave, 'A Soldier of the Great War, Known unto God', was Kipling's own invention.

There the matter rested for another seventy years. Then in 1992, long after both Kiplings and their one surviving daughter were dead themselves, a records officer at the Commonwealth War Graves Commission suggested that an unidentified body marked 'A Lieutenant of the Irish Guards' lying in a grave in an Advanced Dressing Station Cemetery near Loos might be that of John Kipling.

This is no place to go into the exact arguments put forth for this hypothesis, which takes us into the obsessive realm of battle-charts, timings and military insignia. Understandably, the War Graves Commission favours the identification of the nameless dead whenever possible, and the dead Kipling son has become a symbol to represent a multitude. Sufficient to say that by the spring of 1998 the headstone on the grave had had John's name added to it. However, the opinion of several experts whom the Commission themselves had consulted was that the identification was doubtful, and other military experts had got to work on the matter and soon published their views.

Essentially, the arguments against the body being that of John are that: a) it was not found in the right place, given what is known of company movements during the Battle of Loos from day to day; and b) that the relevant body was, from the surviving arm-pips, not a second lieutenant but a full one, as the stone had always stated. The Commission counters this by pointing out that, immediately before his fatal day, John had been listed to go up in rank. However, he would not have had the right to add another pip to his sleeve until the change was official, and would have had no time or opportunity anyway. Further, and most tellingly, it does seem that whoever, in 1919, identified a collection of dead remains from military buttons and badges as belonging to the Irish Guards had got it wrong. The badge concerned was actually the very similar one of the London Irish Rifles – a regiment favoured by the many young men of Irish and Anglo-Irish descent whose families had settled in England.

To quote what had become the standard work on the matter, which has gone into several updated editions since it was first published in 1998:[44] 'Three of the Regiment's officers were killed that day' (that is, 27th September, when John Kipling was last seen, wounded). 'Two have known graves. One is missing, and his name is on the Memorial at Dud Corner, Loos. He is: Lieutenant Arthur Leslie Hamilton Jacob.'

When this conclusion appeared in an article in the *Irish Times* in 2015, a second cousin of mine, who had returned to his family roots in Ireland, contacted me. He sent me the newspaper story, saying, 'I think he must be related to us?' I had been quite unaware of the argument going on and was as surprised by the revelation as he was, but I was able to indicate to him where Arthur Leslie Hamilton Jacob fitted into the Jacob family tree. My cousin realised that 'Leslie' (as he had been known in the family, to differentiate him from his father, Arthur) was an identifiable figure to him, indeed a long-dead uncle.

'I'm sure you're right,' he wrote back to me, 'everything seems to fit. My aunt Kitty had a raft of stuff – the telegram announcing his death, the awful letter from some superior officer saying how bravely he died – your heart goes out to the poor man, who must have had to send out thousands of these things ... and a couple of heart-breaking postcards he [Leslie] had sent from France which read in tone and language – *jolly* and *chums* and *japes* and *tuck* – like the postcards a public schoolboy would send home – I think he signed up with ... his school contemporaries straight from Haileybury.'[45]

My cousin added that his mother, Leslie's much younger sister, had told him that his grandmother 'at one level accepted it [Leslie's death] at the time because of the spirit of patriotic fervour and because everyone was in the same boat, but went to pieces in the 1920s when more evidence of the futility of it all came out'.

He rather thought that all the precious mementoes that his Aunt Kitty, who was Leslie's elder sister, had kept after their mother's death had probably vanished, but subsequent family enquiries located the collection in the possession of yet another cousin, carefully preserved.

DNA testing did not yet exist when the reference to the Irish Guards was put on the headstone above the body, and when the name of John Kipling was added so long afterwards the grave itself was not disturbed. Today, since Kipling and his wife were both cremated, the only possible DNA for comparison lies in the grave of their remaining daughter, who had no children. Since none of us would wish to disturb her, any more than the War Graves Commission feels inclined to dig up the disputed remains, there the matter, like dead bones, rests, probably for ever.

I derive a wry pleasure from thinking that Arthur Leslie, my father's first cousin, who died when he was not yet twenty years old and who had dropped almost completely into that great, quiet dark of oblivion, has now acquired, in the recondite circles of military history, a persistent posthumous renown.

CHAPTER XV

What Will Survive of Us

… there are no voices, O Rhodopé! That are not soon mute, however tuneful: there is no name, with whatever emphasis of passionate love repeated, of which the echo is not faint at last.[46]

In the traditional late-medieval Dance of Death people of all kinds dance in a long chain, conveying the message that mortality is the great leveller. The image is thought to have been inspired by the fourteenth-century Black Death, and to have been given further force by outbreaks of feverish mania in the early sixteenth century that were possibly due to contaminated wheat. Hans Holbein the Younger made a whole series of engravings on what was clearly by then an obsessional theme. Many one-time representations of the Dance on church walls or windows have disappeared – one was deliberately obliterated in London from St Paul's cloister at the Reformation – but some fine examples still exist in small French and German churches and in Eastern Europe. Hand-in-hand they dance, these mortal people representing all walks and conditions of life, but each hand is clasped not by that of another mortal, but by the bony fist of a skeleton: Death is separating each individual from his companions. However, in a few portrayals just two people clasp hands directly with each other. These two, young and fair, are lovers. 'Death,' their unspoken message is, 'cannot separate us. Our love triumphs even over that.'

It was never true, of course. It is a characteristic of romantic passion that the couple believe each other to be unique, and their feeling for each other something beyond the range of ordinary emotion. There are documented stories from both twentieth-century world wars of wives refusing to believe that a husband reported 'missing in action' could actually be dead – 'Because,' reasoned one wife, 'if he were, he would have found the way to get through to me. We promised each other we would, if either of us were killed.' Therefore, her back-to-front desperate optimism concluded, he must be merely lying unidentified in some hospital or in a POW camp. How long she managed to hold on to this illusion is not reported.

Widely known and quoted in support of the belief in love surmounting even death is the last line of Philip Larkin's fine poem 'An Arundel Tomb.' This is about the fourteenth-century Earl of Arundel and his Lady, who lie in life-size effigy in Chichester Cathedral, holding hands, as the 'endless altered people' pass by them:

Our almost-instinct, almost true:
What will survive of us is love.

These lines are displayed today beneath the memorial, but the preceding lines warn of the unreliability of this idea. The verse begins 'Time has transfigured them into untruth', since neither of the Arundels could possibly, in life, have envisaged that their union might become emblematic of enduring love six centuries later. But in addition, what is not mentioned on the monument is that the stone-carved figures have been heavily restored. In the early nineteenth century they were in a battered and crumbling condition, and the restorer[47] used his own judgement in joining their right hands together, in a way unusual in medieval memorials. No other English couple, apparently, are portrayed in this way, though one or two continental examples exist. Long ago, great lords and their ladies did not indulge in public displays of marital affection. Or, if they did, it was not generally thought appropriate to preserve the fact in stone.

The truth about the inevitably finite nature of human attachment is lucidly expressed in Walter de la Mare's well-known poem about a dead, beautiful 'Lady of the West Countree' who was 'light of step and heart':

> But beauty vanishes, beauty passes
> However rare – rare it be –
> And when I crumble who will remember
> This lady of the West Country?

Who indeed? Through this verse she has become an archetype, so one may indeed say that is survival, of a kind. If the original subject was an identifiable individual – and at least one contender has been suggested[48] – this may not necessarily add further meaning to de la Mare's poem, which is essentially about disappearance.

Such is the common lot. But one wonders if the lady perhaps had descendants or celebrated associates, who would keep her name at least alive, along with some scrap of renown passed down through the generations? – 'De la Mare was an admirer of hers, you know.' In such a way, the unknown lady to whom Pierre de Ronsard in the sixteenth century wrote the poem beginning 'Quand vous seriez bien vieille, au soir, à la chandelle … ' ('When you are very old, in the evening, sitting by candle-light … ') has, as he predicted, gained some permanent place in collective memory precisely because he admired her. However, his plea to her at the end of the poem is that she should not fuss about posterity, but enjoy life's transient, flowery pleasures now, in her youth.

The present-day passion for reconstructing family trees, thanks largely to a combination of extensive nineteenth-century record-keeping and the digital possibilities of the twenty-first, inevitably favours those ancestors who procreated over the ones who did not. A several-times-great-grandfather, once triumphantly located, has his place in the great family scheme of things in the way his childless brother or sister never will.

When I was enmeshed at one time, researching a book, in the convoluted toils of a battered, leather-bound volume entitled History of the Families of Jacob from AD. 1275 to 1875, I felt overwhelmed by innumerable Jacob men of every generation, all called Michael, Arthur, Archibald and John. I could hardly find space in my head as well for those who did not actually achieve ancestorhood. And yet I came, almost by chance, upon someone who seems to have had no claim on posterity, and who did nothing publicly remarkable, yet who made her mark in people's hearts to such an extent that some faint essence of her personality became preserved in this book and rises here, like a tiny whiff of a forgotten scent.

She was an Elizabeth Jacob, born in the mid-eighteenth century at Ballinakill, Queen's County, the second of three daughters and six sons of a Michael Jacob. He was a doctor, and was described long after by Elizabeth as being 'a clever medical man and a pleasant companion; his company was sought after by the best in the county'. Maybe this was so, but already this daughter's affectionate and forgiving nature is apparent, since it seems that this Michael Jacob was mysteriously unfair to his children, leaving nearly everything when he died to his wife and to his fourth son, while specifically leaving the other sons only '£5 each for mourning' and arranging for the daughters to have legacies only after their mother's death. One might of course say that the income of a country doctor, however clever and sought-after, would hardly in any case have been sufficient to assure a comfortable life for all, in such a large family.

As it turned out, the son who was the favoured inheritor does not seem to have made anything of his good fortune. He did not become a doctor, and the only thing known about him is that he was a Justice of the Peace, which was a standard part-time role for any local Anglo-Irish minor notable. The leather-bound book that records him and his siblings, and their multifarious ancestors and ever-more-distant cousins, remarks, 'It is probable that the injustice of his father's disposition of his property in his favour had caused family estrangements, which have left us without knowledge of his life. He died unmarried, and we believe that he was intestate, and that the property went eventually amongst his brothers and sisters.' A truly moral story seems to be encapsulated here. It was his brother John who took on the medical practice, moved it to Maryborough (today Portlaoise) and made a success of it. This John was my three-times-great-grandfather, so his sister Elizabeth, whom I calculate to have been about four years older than him, must have been my four-times-great-aunt.

She was apparently known throughout the extended family as 'Aunt Bess', lived a long life and died eventually in Dublin. We are told that ' ... she was a universal favourite from her amiability and good temper, which appear to have been her characteristics even in youth'. (In this, incidentally, she was very different from her brother John, who, though he followed their father in becoming a dedicated country doctor and surgeon, had the reputation of being a tyrant within his own large family.) I have the feeling that Bess, in spite of (or perhaps because of) her qualities, was always something of a maiden aunt designate. She was only in her early thirties when an uncle-by-marriage of hers, who was the rector in Wicklow, wrote to her father in enthusiastic but revealing terms. It seems that Bess had been sent to help out when the rector's household was afflicted by illness. This letter is, unusually, quoted in the leather-bound book, and the rector's initial remarks shock one by their breath-taking condescension: 'the most unexceptionable of her sex that I have ever met with. She knows not how to offend, but is perfectly mistress in the art of universally obliging.'

However, the tone improves in the following paragraph: 'To the sick she is a most constant, delicate and tender attendant – to the healthy she is agreeable as she is compliant, and ready to enjoy and participate that degree of cheerfulness which is the criterion of innocence. It is natural to her to conciliate the good opinion of all who knew her, and I believe every acquaintance she hath may be called her friend.' He ends this paean of praise by describing himself as 'her Lover' – which of course did not mean at all what it would today, but denoted, rather, strong avuncular affection.

Move on another generation or more and a number of pages and, unusually, another letter[49] finds a place in this generally rather dry and close-focused account of who did what professionally and married whom. This letter, written by Aunt Bess herself to an unnamed niece, apparently ended up in the possession of the great-nephew responsible for commissioning and organising the Jacob Families research.

'As I am the oldest one of our family remaining, I wish to tell you my dear niece of our connection, as I find you do not know the half of them. I will begin with my mother ... ' The letter continues with details of a number of eighteenth-century relations, several of whom died in their eighties 'in their perfect reason' and adds at one point, 'They are all dead now.' Evidently Bess was trying to hand on assorted knowledge of which she knew she was the only surviving repository, a theme that tends to resurface for all of us, generation after generation.

> ... Mr Foulkes, my cousin, married a relation of our own ... with whom he got a ten thousand pound fortune. She was a very nice, pretty woman, and well informed ... Her father had been Governor of Bengal for many years, and supported an honourable, humane character, which was in the public prints ... My eldest brother was a clergyman ... but he took it in his head to go and live in England, and it so happened that the Duke of Leeds heard him preach one day, and took such a liking to him that he got acquainted with him (he was reckoned a fine preacher), made him Domestic Chaplain to himself, but the poor fellow took a bad fever and died soon after; he never married ...

Put this with the other part I gave you some time ago, telling you of the other part of our family. I thought to have written this out better, but I could not finish it as I got the paralytic stroke, and makes but a bad hand of writing, but I hope you can read it.

Aunt Bess is said to have died aged eighty-four, much as her long-gone mother and an aunt did. This would put her death around the middle of the 1830s, just before the dawn of the Victorian age with all the change it was to bring. The nephew who was to become my great-great-grandfather was then settled in medical practice in Dublin. Medicine itself, from having been a hit-or-miss affair for centuries, was now evolving into a properly studied science. In another ten years, surgery, with the new boon of anaesthesia, would begin to change out of all recognition. Within the next five years railways would start to spread across England and then across Ireland, too.

Bess did not live to see that, any more than she lived to see the potato famine ravage the countryside where she had lived most of her life, and where another strong-minded John Jacob had inherited the role of country doctor. She is a voice from a world that was over and gone by the time she evoked it, and it has been my privilege to recall her at the last moment, as I once recalled Célestine and her suitors, from the quiet dark of non-being.

CHAPTER XVI

An Unforeseen Afterlife

My life is as light as the lightest bird
On the lightest twig at the edge of the world.
Lightly it hangs like a leaf ready to fall
Gently it floats like paper, shedding its meaning in water.

Another vanished person, another dead aunt perhaps, with a talent for poetic expression but no descendants? Yes. But this one is much closer in time and, by the strange alchemy of fate, her name is known to many more people now than when she died, in her nineties, just before the end of the twentieth century, thinking to disappear entirely:

Strange that my breath still blurs the glass in the window,
And that people can see me coming and hear what I say.
I am no more than a ghost
Hung lightly, lightly
On the hinge of a day.

We have met her before, in another guise. She was my father's sister Monica, the Oxford graduate whose parents were determined she should 'marry well' with someone who could 'give her the standard of living to which she has been brought up'. Blanche, with her impoverished Anglo-Irish dread of her daughter ending up in the same circumstances from which she herself had so thankfully escaped, was, I am sure, the main mover in the remorseless campaign to separate Monica from her beloved, but it was Bertie as 'head of the family' who issued the morally blackmailing ultimatums: 'Do not imagine that your mother and I will ever cease to love you or will cut you off with a shilling, but you must realise that we cannot approve of Brian and never will.' I should never, of course, have known of the ruthlessness with which my grandparents pursued their determination that their only daughter should not marry the young man she had met at Oxford, had that great sagging cardboard carton of their letters, both sent and received, not somehow, quixotically, survived, against all probability.

And there is worse. For Monica, though not in general a hoarder, turned out after her death to have kept every letter Brian had ever written her. Similarly Brian, a portly and lovable schoolmaster by the time I knew him, who had shed most of the signs of his chaotic youth, including his membership of the Communist Party, had kept all Monica's letters to him. In the five years that separated his sudden death from her more lingering one, Monica had clearly done a good deal of throwing away, for there were no mounds of stuff left to us, her younger relatives, to cope with. But she had collected both sets of letters neatly together in one large bureau drawer. She had known it would be me, my brother and our partners who would clear the little house in a lowland Scottish village where she and Brian had spent their last twenty years, and probably me who would deal with these intimate writings.

She wanted me to know, I am sure, what a true love story theirs had been. Yes. But what was inadvertently thus revealed was the mental torment both had suffered, literally for years, before the hurricane of the Second World War blew their own personal lives into a calmer place. At one time Brian, who had no home refuge, not even an unsatisfactory one, since both his parents were dead, and no money since his legal guardian had announced on his twenty-first birthday that he'd had all he could expect, was living in a tent. Such cases are occurring in our own time – but in the 1930s, when minimal lodgings could be had all over the country for a very low rent, it was almost unheard of for anyone with an adequate education to be reduced to coping in this way, especially when he needed to appear clean and respectable enough to hang on to whatever minimally white-collared job he had managed to land. At one point Brian disappeared, feeling that it 'wasn't fair' on the girl he loved to stick to her when this caused her such trouble and grief with her family. On this occasion Monica came rushing back from Canada, where she had been sent to 'get over' Brian, determined to find him and persuade Brian otherwise. Which she evidently did.

A little later, in the mid-1930s, something still more wrenching happened. I cannot be quite sure of this, since not everything was spelt out in so many words, but from what is implied, and from a letter of obscure but abject apology from Brian to Bertie that is in that lethal collection, I think that Monica got pregnant. At a different social level, this would have been the catalyst to lead to a rapid wedding and everyone would have made the best of it. But since Bertie and Blanche moved in medical circles (there was the family medical publishing firm, a Jacob brother who was a doctor, a brother-in-law who was a well-known gynaecologist), another solution evidently offered itself. Monica, I think, was persuaded to have a discreet abortion.

Ten years later, towards the end of the Second World War, when she and Brian were at last married and Brian was with the Army Education Corps in Benghazi (a well-known refuge for Oxford graduates not thought to be exactly dashing soldier types), Monica went into hospital expecting to have a minor surgical procedure to remove the fibroids that caused painful periods and were believed to have been an impediment to conception since their wedding in 1939. She came round from the anaesthetic to find that she had been given a hysterectomy – 'to be on the safe side', the consultant apparently assured her. 'In case anything should turn cancerous.'

'It must have been *terrible* for you,' I said, meaning it. I was twenty-six, and pregnant myself. I had, of course, grown up knowing that 'poor Auntie Monica wasn't able to have children', but had never known the dreadful details of it.

'Yes, it was,' she said quietly. 'But one gets over things, you know. And, with Brian and me both teaching, we always had little boys around us.'

In the last few years of her life, widowed by then, one of her poems reads:

> I have been lucky. My life has held
> Pleasures and joys beyond my best deserving.
> And I have known love. I have loved and been loved
> From my birth until now, the utmost fringe of my days.

I have paid, of course. My heart has been broken,
But broken clean, not chimbled. Now it is mended.
A firmly riveted cup, it serves my turn.

She had always planned to become a writer, though it never worked out in the way she must once have dreamt. Innumerable are those who vaguely plan that destiny for themselves, and many of them do not have either the necessary intelligence or the talent. Yet both of these are evident in the book of carefully copied-out poems that Monica left for me to find, and also in the one novel she did get published. The novel appeared in 1946: both Brian's absence towards the end of the war and the closing-of-the-door on the possibility of motherhood seem to have created a space in her mind to work on the project. The book was called *The Late Mrs Prioleau*, and its memorable first line runs: 'The first and only time I saw my mother-in-law was when she lay dead in her coffin.'

It is clear from the family tensions portrayed in the book, and the agonising, long-drawn-out and finally failed love-affair at its heart, that Monica's decade-long Calvary of frustrated love and hope concerning Brian fed into it, in essence, though not in any literal way. In other respects the plot and setting of the story derive from the last era of Anglo-Irish gaiety before the Troubles and the Independence movement set in, a period she never knew herself, but knew so well from her mother Blanche's stories of the lost Dublin world. The family in the book are not doctors, but occupy the same not-quite-landed-gentry position as the Jacob clan. They own (till disaster strikes, in the form of religious mania) a prosperous whiskey distillery – 'Crawfurds Mountain Dew'.

Monica, as we know, loved her mother and was much distressed at the years'-long battles with her over Brian. She appreciated Blanche's capacity for gaiety, her amusing and vivid anecdotes, the hospitable welcome she gave to relatives near and far. The ageing, vituperative mother-in-law, whom the narrator of *The Late Mrs Prioleau* gets to know at second hand through disquieting stories and a discovered journal, is clearly not a recognisable portrait of Blanche. Yet, even as a child on occasional visits to that set of grandparents, I sensed that Granny could be quite tiresome, sometimes deliberately combative. Relations between her and my own mother were edgy, to say the least, though that was no doubt my mother's fault as much as Blanche's. Long after Blanche's death, when we were talking family matters, Monica once said to me of Blanche, 'Oh – Mother was a destroyer … ' I was too struck by this intense and out-of-character remark to ask further questions, as perhaps she hoped I would, and now all who might cast further light on this are dead and gone themselves.

The Late Mrs Prioleau is so accomplished, in characterisation and sense of place, in spite of what Monica herself once described to me as its 'rather weak plot construction', that why, one wonders, were there no more novels? I think part of the answer lies in the fact that, while many would-be writers have more ambition than talent, in Monica the qualities were reversed. She had the talent, she could have developed it further – but the private ruthlessness, and the capacity to prioritise writing over other demands, were lacking. Once, two or three years before her death, when I was visiting her in the now-quiet little house not far from the Solway Firth, she told me that a fairground fortune-teller had once said to her: 'You have great gifts, but you will waste them.' She added, 'Of course I never believed in silly things like that. But now I do ask myself what I've done with my life ... '

She was always admiring and supportive of my own writing career, but slightly puzzled as to how I did it. Fairly late in her life she twice gave me further manuscript novels of her own to read. Both times I wrote a report myself, as if for a publisher, but let Monica think these reports had come from a professional reader of my acquaintance. That seemed more tactful, and easier on our relationship.

I could see clearly why these books did not really work: Monica had, simply, enjoyed herself too much writing about some peripheral characters and had not done the research necessary to make other key ones convincing. In the relief and happiness of being with Brian, comfortably occupied (unlike many wives of her generation) teaching the youngest ones in the sheltered community of a boys' boarding school, her life no longer simply had the necessary grist to make the mill-wheels of creativity turn. There was also a confounding notion that she and Brian might write 'joint detective stories': she evidently didn't want him to feel left out. Naturally, since Brian was not really a writer, nothing came of that.

And yet, and yet ... As she aged she took to writing poetry. Obscurely, with little idea of how or where she might get this published. And in some of these copied-out poems she left for me there survives, it seems to me, the authentically unsparing tone of the born writer:

This is the end of the road. The Ivory Gates
Crumble from dubious hinges, black fog shutters

The distant Delectable Mountains;
The Waters of Comfort run dry …

… Our guide has left us. His disembodied smile
Hangs in the air. And fades.
His reassuring voice dissolves. In gibberish.
Our comfortable tour ends in a wilderness

Littered with broken toys
Where there is no hotel,
No one to help us with the luggage,
No luxury bus to Utopia.

Other lines evoke briefly biblical images from the Book of Ecclesiastes, Chapter 12, of 'the broken wheel' and 'leaking cistern'. It is clear that Monica was imbued with the imagery from the St James's Bible that was the inheritance of most of her generation, and of all the generations lying behind them – and also that she had, like many of her contemporaries, discarded the entire panoply of faith. The waters of comfort had indeed run dry for her, yet the poem indicates that this, in itself, was a subject for obscure distress, a sense of loss. Probably the issue of going to church, or not, had been another bone of contention between her and her traditionally believing parents.

When Brian's fatal heart attack occurred, Monica and he, who had always been enthusiastic foreign travellers, were on a last, rather ill-planned holiday in Madeira. It fell to me to fly out to organise a funeral there and bring Monica home. Madeira, with its long tradition from sailing-ship days of being first-stop-out for world travellers and last-stop-before-home, still has a British chaplain in residence. He, and other helpful people, were well used to inopportune British deaths there. I said to Monica that I thought we should just go along with the regular funeral service that was on offer, and she docilely agreed this would be the simplest way. She was longing to get herself, and her grief, home. But immediately before the funeral she said to me: 'Dear, will you ask the vicar not to say anything about the Life Everlasting? Because Brian and I don't believe in that sort of tosh.'

Since the Church of England service commonly begins, '"I am the Resurrection and the Life", saith the Lord, "and he that believeth in me, though he may die, shall live"' this request was rather hard to fulfil. Fortunately Monica's deafness, plus her disinclination to use her hearing aid (she had always been able to hear Brian's stentorian schoolmaster's tones), and also a healthy shot of whisky just before the ceremony, more or less solved the problem. Nor, I think, did she ever contemplate the poignant irony that Brian, a lifelong unbeliever with no pretensions at all to personal renown, was henceforth to lie among some famous names in one of the best-known Anglican cemeteries in the world.

'He was such a nice man. We were all so fond of him,' I said to her in Madeira.

'Yes. He was a nice man. But you know, dear, he was getting rather odd. And forgetful. Really, it was time he was gone ...'

Monica's only voiced hope for herself was that she should be 'kindly remembered' – a modest ambition, considering that it extinguishes like a tiny spark when the last of the rememberers themselves are gone. She was well aware that certain other figures from our family, including my own mother (her sister-in-law), were not gently and readily remembered. She thought this sad, but understandable. I think she would like to know – but I don't suppose she does – that an old but rather good-quality leather handbag like a miniature satchel, which she had mainly used to carry about the house her cigarettes, lighter, small change and a handkerchief, is now with me and has led a whole new life.

It accompanies me to literary, historical or architectural gatherings where I don't want to be burdened with a heavier bag. It has been with me to No. 10 Downing Street, when I was summoned to be polite in French to visiting politicians; it has come with me to the French embassy and to the BBC; to book-signings, to Paris and to Amsterdam. It has sat on my lap through numerous plays and films. It has even had a replacement zip carefully inserted – at a cost probably much more, when not adjusted for inflation, than its original price. Fortunate bag, to have such a prolonged and valued existence.

But that is not quite the end of the story as you might suppose.

I believed for decades – when I thought about it, which was not very often – that *The Late Mrs Prioleau* was one of those innumerable dead-and-gone novels that the twentieth century produced, and would remain as such. I felt as if I was the only person – apart from one or two close relatives on whom I had pressed my one cherished copy ('Mind you give it back!') – who even knew of its existence.

But in our new digital times a book that has lain dormant for half a century can be rediscovered by a bibliophile somewhere in the world and brought back to life again. And not even to its old life, but a new, enhanced one freighted with a 'period' appeal and historical dimension to which it did not originally aspire.

So it came about that *Mrs Prioleau* was republished in 2017 by a small English reprint house, in a paperback with an attractive cover resembling the original one, and also as an e-book.[50] To my gratified surprise, these have been gently selling. The royalties, correctly marked in the quarterly statements as 'unearned income', come to me. As my brother did not quite live to see this happy rebirth, the copyright has ended up with me alone.

I would love to think that, as with the new life of her handbag, Monica somehow, somewhere, in some place outside time, knows of this rebirth, of the continuing existence of something she 'did' with her life. But, as with my brother's fantasy of becoming a Victorian train-driver, I rather doubt if this is the case.

CHAPTER XVII

The Arcades of the Rue de Rivoli

There is another figure besides Monica who has lurked on the fringes of this book, complicating the picture like an image of the same person in a clouded mirror. She too felt herself destined to be a writer. She was only a couple of years younger than Monica, and from a similar comfortably-off bourgeois home, enlightened enough to let a girl go to Oxford. There, she too met the young man who was to become her husband, but it was her good fortune that this young man was from an appropriate background with good financial prospects. He was, in fact, Monica's younger brother. This girl was, of course, my mother, Ursula.

From a few passing references in this account, readers will know that she died prematurely, in circumstances customarily described as 'tragic', when I was on the verge of adulthood and her son, my brother, N, was not quite nine. It should not, however, be supposed that some disastrous event, grief or a series of them precipitated her shocking end. It is common, and no doubt understandable, for bystanders to such a drama to seek some identifiable reason for a suicide. People seem to feel reassured if they can ascribe such an act to 'money worries' or 'a failed love-affair', 'professional disappointment', 'not being happy living in the country' or even to such an inadequate notion as 'mid-life crisis' – as if such experiences, with variations, were not part of the common lot, regularly surmounted, with pain but without drama, by innumerable people who go on to live out a full lifespan. Others, in the harsher places on Earth, suffer far more appalling experiences, often entailing the loss of home, all possessions and everything they have held dear, even their children, yet rarely kill themselves in consequence. Clearly the suicidal impulse is its own phenomenon, and the undoubted strength and persistence of the urge towards it seems to bear little relation to the actual life-circumstances of the person so obsessed.

Over the years that followed my mother's death, I occasionally had well-intentioned relatives or old family friends officiously suggesting that I should 'remember her as she used to be – before All That started'. 'All That' was the period of three to four years that preceded her death, during which she admitted herself that something was wrong, but stridently insisted it was 'just the change of life'. She seemed to view this as some unavoidable blight that set in promptly at age forty and was no respecter of personality – 'It's like flu, you see,' she insisted to me. 'It can happen to anyone.' She had not in fact reached the menopause, and anyway I was becoming uneasily aware by that time that something more general and longer-term than malfunctioning hormones was wrong with Ursula and with her perception of the world and of herself.

Let us return to the happy, fortunate girl she once was. She had an indulgent, not-very-intellectual mother, and a

distinguished father who ended a long and varied career as a
Treasury knight. She had an affectionate brother near in age, as
her childhood companion. She grew up in a pleasant riverside
outer-London suburb surrounded by other families of a similar
kind. She wrote engaging little magazines, copies of which her
mother lovingly kept. She learnt to play tennis well. At about
twelve she was sent to a prestigious girls' boarding school and
seems to have thrived there. ('Oh, I loved my boarding school,'
she would say to me, with the implication 'Of course you will
too.') She was genuinely an avid reader and, having been
well educated, and with her father as a recommendation, she
seems to have been accepted at one of the then-women's colleges
in Oxford without difficulty. It was towards the end of her first
term there, skating on a frozen sheet of water at the onset of a
famously cold winter, that she literally bumped into my father,
also in his first term. Ursula was not especially pretty, but she
was slim, vivid, energetic, articulate – and determinedly 'modern',
that byword of the 1920s and '30s. By their third year at university the pair were engaged to be married.

Both sets of parents, I have been told, thought them too
young and urged them to wait, but apart from that, there were
no obvious objections. Unlike his college-friend Brian, who was
already in trouble over Monica, my father, 'Tim', with his nice
manners, place booked in the family medical publishing business
and essentially conventional outlook, was obviously a suitable
son-in-law, from the perspective of Ursula's parents. On the
other side, if Blanche had some justified reservations about this
Thoroughly Modern Girl who was taking her adored son from
her, I rather think that Ursula's impressive father, plus a more
distant eminent Huguenot ancestor or two, reassured her. And

anyway they couldn't marry just yet, could they, as they couldn't afford to until Bertie made Tim a partner in the firm … ?

However, in early spring 1934 Tim and Ursula entered, just for fun and fashionableness, a lottery for a substantial betting-ticket on a racing horse. Lotteries were illegal in England then, but not in Ireland: this one, indeed, was the Irish Sweep. They drew a lucky ticket with a horse's name on it: Golden Miller. That year Golden Miller won the Grand National. Even though the young couple had hedged their bet, on standard advice, by selling off half the ticket, they still won many thousands of pounds – a fortune, in today's terms.

It is hardly surprising, in the circumstances, that this undeservedly but supremely lucky golden-boy-and-girl insisted on marrying that same summer. They must have felt that Fate had taken a personal interest in them and that the world was at their feet.

So what, you may well wonder, went so horribly wrong that, twenty-one years, two children and a world war later, Ursula walked out of a carefully chosen new home in London into which they had just moved from Sussex ten days earlier? It was a foggy autumn day, very early in the morning. She took with her a pack of barbiturates (readily prescribed in those days before modern anti-depressants) and succeeded in shutting herself into a little-used garage, which then appeared locked. It took three days of frantic searching, in a place where, because of the house-move, we knew no one, before she was found.

All suicidal people are self-absorbed, that is their curse. It is useless to complain of that – but Ursula's final act has always seemed to me fairly far up the scale of the self-absorbed spectrum. She left no note, no word of love or apology. Not for her

husband, who had spent the last four years desperately trying
to 'understand' and to support her emotionally. Not for her little
boy, sent away by then for his first, bleak year at a distant
boarding prep-school. Not for her mother or her very old and
always-adored father. And not for me, who had, when younger,
been the centre of her existence. She did not even wait to find
out if I had got into the college for which, a few weeks earlier,
between packing up our old house and helping my father
organise the new one, I had sat the entrance exam.

Not till I had a young child of my own did I allow myself
fully to realise what a betrayal of love and trust it is for a mother
to turn her back on her small son. And not till our own son
was big did I let myself realise how much I, too, had been marked
by her abandonment of me.

This is not a very kind portrayal of someone who was clearly
in the grip of an irrational depression. But the sad fact is that
too much 'understanding', without any adequate explanation of
what was supposed to be the matter, was asked of me in my
early teens, a time when nature pushes one in the opposite
direction. Exiled to a third-rate girls' boarding school for much
of the year, where I did not thrive, it came as a huge relief when
my tearfully adamant refusal to return there for yet another
year was taken seriously. In any case, my presence at home was
becoming rather necessary. But, cooking and shopping in the
intervals between the tutorial classes I now attended, I found
myself also expected to keep a watch on a mother who kept
collapsing into bed for no clearly defined reason. I was told to
explain to the rare guests that she was suffering from migraine,
which I knew to be a fabrication. I listened patiently to endless

computations of how much sleep she thought she had 'missed' by lying awake at night, as if sleep were some sort of bank balance and she was owed by right a debt of hours, which must somehow be made up.

I was told by my genuinely sleep-deprived and increasingly desperate father, as he disappeared for his morning train to town, 'Try not to leave Mummy alone too much.' But he never said exactly what it was that I was supposed to prevent happening. I conclude that he was too terrified of the possibility to give it a name. And perhaps he took refuge in the cosy folk-myth that 'People who talk about killing themselves never actually do.'

I behaved 'well' and quietly prided myself on the fact. I thought: 'At least I'm grown-up now.' Having absorbed the mantra that one simply mustn't ask, 'Why can't Mummy pull herself together?' I got the impression that I wasn't allowed even to think it. In this way, I suppose, my inevitably limited adolescent capacity for compassion was overstrained and, like a young animal worked too hard before it has its full strength, that capacity has never fully recovered. I know this is a failure in me, and I regret it. But I also know, with my adult experience and intellect, that all the uncritical 'understanding' in the world could not, in itself, have saved my mother from the pit she had dug for herself, whereas a tougher and more challenging approach from someone, years earlier, when she would have been more receptive, might have significantly altered the course of things for her.

Arguably, what this self-deluding woman – who is today more than young enough to be my daughter – needed was someone like my present-day self to bully and care for her. Alas!

*

The well-meant encouragement to me to 'try to remember your mother as she was', rather than how her life ended, was anyway impossible. Death, a French saying goes, transforms a life into a destiny. When the picture is completed in a violent way, that simple fact alters the perception of the whole. A young man dying in a war becomes for ever a dead, lost hero; any tendency he had to quarrel with his brother or be rude to his mother becomes an irrelevancy. Just so, too, the wife, mother, potential grandmother who betrays everyone's love and trust by her sudden abandonment of her own future, and everyone else's, is for ever perceived in that ultimate role. We all know that the past affects our view of what may be to come, but it is perhaps less often observed that later events may shed a permanently altered light on the recollection of earlier ones.

One early-twentieth-century novelist took this perception to an extreme, in a haunting tale that shows the originally innocent memories of happiness in youth irreparably sullied by the taint of a single later event. This was May Sinclair, who was born in 1863, but who only seems to have begun writing in middle life, in the years before and immediately after the First World War, when all sorts of new perceptions were afoot. She died, largely forgotten, in 1946, but by the time I came upon her a generation later, interest in her work was once again stirring. Her novella, *Where Their Fire Is Not Quenched*, opens with the peaceful death of an apparently blameless woman who, long ago, had one guilty affair with a married man. Life-after-death for her turns out to be an endless recapitulation of originally innocent experiences and relationships, all of which have now become distorted and contaminated by her Sinful one. Again and again, with the authentic sense of a bad dream, she finds herself reliving a happy fieldside tryst as a young girl, or later blameless friendships, or her old-age contentment as deaconess to an adored vicar, but each time the decor of the dream begins subtly to change and once again she is back in Paris, in front of a particular hotel, and it is her secret partner in Sin that she is, after all, to meet.

For her, it is the grey arcades of a hotel in the rue de Rivoli, that well-established venue for adulterous Anglo-Saxon liaisons, that intrudes on remembered, previous happiness. For me, another place. I am not, of course, making any moral equivalence between suicide and adultery: they are obviously quite different versions of betrayal. I am simply indicating the capacity of one bad experience to spread its destruction retrospectively as well as subsequently. For very many years, the rare times when I consciously tried to recall all the happy experiences of my childhood rather than the troubling ones – the walks on Ashdown Forest, where my mother and I regularly dammed a stream together; the morning of my brother's birth; the kittens and the guinea pigs that populated my childhood; the ha'pennies provided for the railway-line game; the stories, poetry and, later, grown-up novels to which my mother introduced me; her help in editing an early story of mine; the occasion when she bought me my own choice (not hers) of an expensive and beautiful dress and asked me not to mention the price to my father ... When I tried to enumerate these things to myself, it was another place to which memory carried me. A shut garage with three successive chilly autumn dawns coming in through a high window. An oil-stained cement floor, a water jug, a glass and an empty pack of pills.

So, what did go so horribly wrong? Two combined reasons suggest themselves, one simple, the other a little more recondite.

In the first place, it seems clear that my mother's growing-up was just too fortunate and sheltered to give her any practice at all in coping with adversity or even with not getting her own way. Her kind mother, the granny I knew best, was indulgent to a fault, and Ursula was her father's favourite child. He was, I think, unimpressed by his rather gentle only son, preferring my mother, whom he felt had inherited much of his intellect. He had had clever sisters, who had made their way in life even in the late nineteenth century by their own abilities and confidence; so should his daughter. Modern feminist assumptions regarding attitudes to girls at that time, as applied to this privileged girl, are quite out of place. She was not required to learn to cook or clean, there were servants for that, but nor was she required to go to church, sit and sew or any other such occupation that was now, in the conscious, post-1918 world of modernity, regarded as 'Victorian'. There were none of the stern punishments or tedious governesses that were still sometimes to be found in such households then, but pleasant schooldays in well-chosen establishments and holidays in the Isle of Wight and Brittany, bike rides and eventually driving lessons. When she came down from Oxford with a not-very-distinguished degree, Ursula was not required to be 'a girl at home', as many of her generation still were, but was enabled, with financial assistance, to scale the excitingly modern heights of a job in London and a flat there, shared with an Oxford friend. It seems clear that young Ursula had enjoyed a quite extraordinarily sheltered and fortunate existence, which had fostered in her that sense of entitlement that is not necessarily a useful preparation for the long haul of living.

She had not even undergone the common experience of an unhappy love-affair. Meeting Tim near the beginning of her time at Oxford, and marrying him so triumphantly, thanks to Golden Miller, she seems to have assumed both that they would be Happy Ever After in the traditional way, and that they would also be a Thoroughly Modern Couple leading a life characterised by cocktail-parties, visits to the theatre and 'pâté sandwiches off the mantelpiece at midnight'. While Tim went dutifully into the family firm, she would become a novelist.

Ursula was not a fool, or without talent. She had a good ear for dialogue, and in her first two novels, published before I was born and reviewed as 'light, modern and amusing', she satirised exactly that sort of life, complete with the pâté sandwiches. When a hint of trouble appeared – Tim, though he believed Ursula to be a stronger and cleverer person than him, was susceptible, and also attractive to other women – they decided to have a baby, and moved from a flat into a proper house near Regent's Park.

I was born in the year of the Munich crisis. Nannies were engaged, who came and went. My parents were too innocent, it seems, to understand for over fifteen months (when it was pointed out to them by the army) that it had been their responsibility to register my birth: as a result, my birth certificate looks a little odd to this day. By that time it was obvious, even to this feckless young couple, that another war was coming. Tim, like many others, joined up as a reservist to pre-empt the expected call-up. London life was abandoned – or, rather, was abandoning them. Ursula took me to stay first with her own parents in

Sussex, and then to share a house with the family of an old college friend, thus retreating into girlhood again. It was, I have been told, in the autumn of 1939 that my father held me on his lap for the last time, as I crawled over him in his new lance corporal's uniform, apparently noting with pleasure his buttons and badges. Soon afterwards he was sent to the Middle East. We were not to meet again till 1944 and, as he admitted long after, he never, perhaps because of this long break, developed much paternal feeling. His attitude to me indeed always seemed more like that of an uncle towards a favourite niece rather than one of fundamental responsibility.

At this point we come to the other, more elusive reason for Ursula's ultimate failure at living.

Among the many theories as to why some people in every society take their own lives is one advanced, almost as a subsidiary thought to his central analysis, by the sociologist Émile Durkheim.[51] Some people, in his view, seek death as the ultimate, dramatic change because they have failed to achieve a whole series of changes in life's normal course. When I first read this, in my late twenties, it came to me as an illumination in a dark place. I had noticed, since my childhood, that Mummy seemed ill-at-ease in the post-war world and used to talk wistfully about 'the dear old days' and 'when things get back to normal again', which other adults that I knew did not. I had not previously considered that the personal capacity for development and change varies considerably from one individual to another, but now, when I came to reflect upon it as an adult, I realised that what especially characterised Ursula both during the war and afterwards was her marked failure to evolve and adjust.

Tim started the war as a silly young man who took a while to get a commission because his superiors did not think much of him. He ended it having seen service in Palestine, in the Western Desert, in the Monte Cassino battles that followed the Salerno landings, and finally as part of the follow-up army to the Normandy landings, driving the enemy back through France and Belgium and into Germany. He was by now a captain, acting major, well respected, with his own staff car and driver and huge amounts of experience under his belt. It was, of course, hard on my mother to have several years without him, but she was far from being the only wife in this position. Dads were usually 'away fighting the Germans', in my young experience, and many wives were able to put the war to use as an opportunity for personal growth, publicly or more privately. Even within our own limited Sussex circle, I knew other mummies who worked in canteens, or as voluntary nurses in the local hospital that was full of badly burnt airmen, or on farms. Mummies taught in schools or sat on local councils or organised Infant Welfare Clinics and evacuee services. One upper-class mother of a small school-friend of mine actually drove the van daily for the farmer who distributed most of the local milk, as his van-man had been called up. (It was a treat to me and her own daughter to be fetched from school in the van, even though the sour smell of ancient milk-spillings was overpowering.)

My mother could have done any of these things. She had only one child, me, and for two years she had been living more or less as a guest in the household of her married college friend. When we moved back to Sussex, in spite of the war there was always a nanny or a housekeeper. She also had her parents, my grandparents, living nearby. She could have done almost anything useful that appealed to her: she could even have gone up to London several days a week, had that been indicated. Instead, she sat at home waiting for the war to be over, for things to 'get back to normal' and to be successful and amusing and Modern once again. After one good further novel about a village at the outbreak of war, the sources of creation began to dry. She went on writing, but her limited store of personal experience, to which she had added so little, was almost used up. The novel she published at the end of the war, her last one, was set again in 1939, and who wanted to read about that in 1945? One reviewer, more percipient than others in those rather thin times for literature, remarked that 'all Ursula Orange's heroines seem to have "1930" stamped between their shoulder blades'.

Is it perhaps significant that, in spite of her good education, Ursula's grasp of history was oddly inadequate? The woman who had studied all Shakespeare's history plays at Oxford with genuine enthusiasm for blank verse seemed largely unaware of their wider context. I also recall my priggish fifteen-year-old self being shocked to discover that she could not locate the industrial revolution in time: she apparently thought it might be encapsulated in the phrase 'the Hungry Forties'. Nor was she any repository of family history, although this classically tends to be a female role. I recall my uncle, her brother, once referring to some amusing family story associated with a distant great-aunt from Yorkshire, but Ursula's reaction was a dismissive 'Oh goodness, I think it's time we forgot about her, don't you?'

It is not she who would ever have amassed a little collection of talismans, survivors from a vanished past. She was a brisk thrower-awayer. No saved letters surfaced after her death, no sign that she had valued any memento. Perhaps it is partly because of this that I, in turn, kept nothing of hers. I inherited her jewellery, including her engagement ring and a black opal ring – a sinister possession, some would say, since in past times these were regarded as mourning rings. I no longer have the rings, or other jewellery of hers. I believe I sold it all decades ago, though I have kept pieces inherited from Blanche, and from Monica. So there is no object, in this last chapter, that speaks of Ursula.

I had, for a while, a thick, dark-blue cable-knit jersey she had knitted for me, and that I continued to wear at university on cold days, but at some point I must have given it away to a charity shop. Now, I think I would not do so. But this was Then. I avoided ever thinking about her.

My father had finally come home for good in 1945, no more adjusted to the post-war world than she was, and with the family firm to get back on course. He should, no doubt, have done more to force Ursula into the present than he did. They should, among other things, have had a proper conversation then, rather than ten years later, about whether it was really a good idea to stay in Sussex. But this – with a long daily commute to London by steam-train – was apparently part of Tim's inherited concept of married life. Perhaps Ursula was resigned to pleasing him in this, after all their years apart and the various wartime love affairs that she must have suspected he had had on leaves in Cairo and 'Alex'; and anyway quite soon the new baby was on the way ... And everyone knew that 'the country' was the correct place to bring up children.

They had a full-time nanny again, which many middle-class families by then did not. At the very least, once my brother was safely born, Ursula might have gone up to London quite often to keep Tim company for an evening out and to reconnect with old friends, but, for whatever reason, this did not happen. Instead, she took refuge and solace in an outdated idea of herself as 'unconventional' and 'progressive', for which the Sussex outer-commuter belt did not provide a great deal of scope. In practice, her grasp of current affairs was weak and her natural tendencies nervously Conservative, but she sought out one or two eccentric old school-friends whom she felt were somehow leading more enlightened lives than she was.

She also rejected the local Protestant convent school, which is where the other small girls like me were sent from the age of about eight, and tried to insert me successively into two progressive establishments. One, a Rudolf Steiner school full of people whose accents I could not understand, was so alien to me in its eccentric authoritarianism – one was not allowed to read till double teeth had come through; one was made to paint on wet paper – that for the first but not the last time in my life I refused, with screams and tears, to go back there. So she took me away and, after a while, sent me to a still more eccentric establishment on the edge of Ashdown Forest, a school run on A.S. Neill lines, but without the personality and talent of Neill to give it force. It was, in effect, a hippy-commune *avant le jour*. All the staff were, I came to understand, members of The Party: I wondered vaguely what that might be? Lessons were optional, and anyway there were no proper lessons as such: lots of model-making, made-up drama and dancing, but no maths, grammar, history or languages. I remember thinking that it was lucky I already knew (approximately) how to read and write, since I could not see how the smaller children, corralled in a playroom near the kitchen, were ever going to acquire these skills.

Everyone was a boarder except me, and I spent my time nervously concealing the fact that the home I returned to each afternoon had a cloth laid for tea and a nanny. No one was exactly nasty to me, but I didn't fit in and spent many hours alone reading the old bound copies of *Punch* with which the battered and scarcely furnished house was plentifully supplied – and thereby, I suspect, acquiring a lifetime's interest in social history. In that mythical period Before the War the place had been a gentleman's country house. My grandmother told me that she remembered, when she and my grandfather were newly retired to Sussex, being invited to dinner there.

After two years of this, it occurred to my mother – or just possibly my father, emerging for once from publishing concerns and proof-correcting – that I was unlikely in such a milieu ever to pass any useful exams. I was hastily removed, and sent for an enjoyable summer of necessary remedial coaching to a local vicar who specialised in such things. My companions there were three boys being hauled through Common Entrance. I made haste to forget the explicit language that was casual currency in the pre-hippy establishment, sensing that it would not be appropriate. I was then sent to the overcrowded girls' private boarding school in another one-time gentry house. It had no proper sixth form, no track-record in university entrance, no science teaching at all, no gym, no library, no common rooms and a totally inadequate provision of bathrooms – all defects which I can only assume Ursula was by then too absorbed in her own outdated fantasy world to notice.

She resented being 'stuck' in Sussex, she resented having to cook (though she did it quite competently, and taught me how to make a stew, a necessary basic skill for life). She mourned the loss of the slim figure that she thought had been hers as of right, but it did not seem to occur to her to take up again the riding, tennis or swimming that, in earlier years, she had enjoyed. The image of the other, 'real', more desirable life that had been hers, but which she was somehow unfairly prevented now from leading, dominated her imagination.

It was not that she did not try. She sold a story or two to a women's magazine. She spent much time and energy compiling an anthology of poems that might appeal to a group that had then hardly been identified – teenagers. She produced a fine finished typescript, with comments on the poems and their authors, plus a set of pictures drawn by an eccentrically artistic friend of hers. But all this work came to nothing, since she had not thought to get it commissioned beforehand. Why, I now ask myself? She was familiar with publishing; she should have known that discussion with a publisher is a first step with such a book. Come to that, Tim must have known, too, and should have told her to go up to London and talk to someone about it. Perhaps he did and she didn't listen. Further vistas of unreality appear in her grasp of ordinary life.

She had another idea. She got very interested in the poet Shelley and in both his wives. This was in fact, as I only now realise, an inspired concept, well in advance of its time. She did a good deal of research, and if only she had followed this up by writing a proper biography, which she was in many ways well equipped to do, this could have brought her back into the literary circles and the prestige that she craved. But an infatuation with the theatre, dating (of course) from Before the War when she had known several actors, led her to turn her research into a play instead. As she knew nothing about dramatic construction, which functions quite differently from novel-writing, and seldom ventured up to London to the theatre any more, this initiative failed, too. Further distress, further sense, no doubt, of self-worthlessness.

As a final throw of the dice, it was at last agreed that we should move back to London, something eagerly endorsed by me, since the attractions of country living did not mean much any more to the frustrated, lonely teenager I had become. For a while the finding of a suitable house, and the plans for arranging and furnishing it, seemed to distract my mother from her increasing inertia, her 'change-of-life problems' and her obsession that somehow she was being denied adequate sleep and many other things to which she felt she was entitled. She believed that in London everything would be different. She would find again her 'real' self, the talented, fortunate girl she had once been.

We already know how disastrously that enterprise ended.

There is, however, a corollary to this story, just as there is to Monica's.

Sometime in 2016 it was brought to my attention that an American blog put out by someone styling himself *furrowedmiddlebrow*, with a particular interest in novels of the first half of the twentieth century, had made a reference to more than one of my mother's books. He seemed especially keen on what was in fact the best, the one set in a village at the outbreak of war, which had been published in the States as well as in Britain, and he was puzzled that he could find out nothing more about the author. For a while, I lay low.

But then another reader wrote into the blog, revealing that he had read one of my own books, *Footprints in Paris*, and from a short section in this had deduced that my mother was Ursula Orange. My disguise had been thin; I had not been expecting my mother to come back from the dead in this way. But at this point I thought it best to reveal myself.

Furrowed Middlebrow and I eventually met, in London, and the long and the short of it was that no fewer than three of Ursula's six novels were eventually republished, by the same reprint house[52] that was to take on *The Late Mrs Prioleau*, and on the same terms. Would I like, I was asked, to write a foreword to them, as I had for Monica's book? No, actually, I would not. I knew I could not trust myself to be fair. But I suggested for the job someone else, an old friend with whom I had worked briefly once before on a project and who, I knew, had a particular interest in such things. She indeed brought to the three novels the keen eye, the generosity and open-mindedness that I was unable to summon.

I owe to her the perception that my mother's aborted idea of writing about Mary Shelley was, indeed, a strikingly original and good one for the early 1950s, something that I had failed to notice. She also remarked on how touching and obviously authentic were the successive pictures in my mother's novels of a small girl – me, at varying ages. And that these are word-portraits by someone who really loved her child, observed her, cared for her and entered into a child's world in a way many mothers cannot, or won't.

> Our almost-instinct, almost true:
> What will survive of us is love.

My love for Ursula has not survived. It died, I think, with her on that cold garage floor. But, through time and chance, a record of her love for me has survived, against all the odds, and now reappears again. Her books form, after all, a lasting testimony that can present a slice of recent, yet so-distant social history to a generation of which she did not dream.

The three chosen novels, like *The Late Mrs Prioleau*, are selling gently but steadily. I am really pleased for her.

But what of my abandoned little brother, N? As he once pointed out to me, long after we were both grown-up and indeed middle-aged, within one year he had lost the entire setting of his young life – not only (*only?*) his mother, but the home and village he had always known, and also the day-school where he had been happy and had flourished. His life could hardly have been changed more completely, had he been a refugee transported to a new country.

There had, of course, been ominous signs beforehand, but he had been too young to interpret them. In recent holiday times he had had me looking after him rather a lot, and a teenage sister with her own preoccupations is a poor substitute for a mother. Then there came a time, in the last year of Ursula's life, when he had been parked for much of one term in the home of some boy cousins, one of them near his own age, and had temporarily gone to their school. Many years later they remembered him as a 'rather alarmingly good little boy'. Understandably perhaps, if sadly, he never sought much subsequent contact with them.

After our mother's body was found, I accompanied our father on the long drive to N's boarding school, where he had been for only one term and a bit, to 'break the news' to him. We did not bring him back to London with us for at least a few days, as we should have done. Evidently our father was too disorientated by what had happened to take proper responsibility for his little boy ('The school will look after him, I'm sure ...') and I can only suppose that I was too intent on holding myself together to protest at this, as I should have done.

Our father, who could never bear to be without female company, bolted all too soon from his own grief (and hence emotionally from both his children, too) into a hasty and rather unsuitable second marriage. Quietly horrified at this turn of events, I escaped into what I took to be adulthood – a state that by persistence, trial and chance, and a fortunate degree of inborn resilience, some years later I did more or less achieve.

And what of N? This book began with him, and it seems right to close with him, too.

With his father retreating into the favourite old role of young-man-in-love, his sister desperately putting together her own new life as best she could, his real mother gone and never mentioned, and the new substitute too unsophisticated, too childishly protective of her own position and too generally incompetent and lazy-minded to take on the demanding role of stepmother to a bereaved child – what of N in all this destruction?

Unsurprisingly, he who had been a most able and promising pupil in his first few years at school ceased to flourish. Neither at his lonely prep boarding school, nor in the bleakness of the famous public school to which he was later sent, did he thrive. Worse, he developed a persistent skin disease, like a permanent case of adolescent acne, over much of his body, sore and disfiguring, an intolerable shirt of flame ...

This must look as if it is going to turn into one of those depressing case-histories, full of breakdowns, with a large dollop of psychoanalytical assumptions about how all the later ills of a life can be ascribed to bad early experiences, etc., etc. ... But it isn't.

I never said anything to N about how inadequate I thought our stepmother was. I felt, maybe hoped, that as she was the only mother he had, perhaps he had developed some fondness for her. Not till she was safely dead, a great many years later, did I discover, in one of the first frank conversations I had ever had with him, that his opinion of her had been similar to mine. 'Look what she's done,' he said, 'to Our Mutual Father. It is bad for an intelligent man to be tied to a ninny like that.'

For by some wonderful chemistry, luck or good genes, N, in spite of his tragic childhood, eventually grew up eminently sane. It took him a good while, but he achieved it, along with a more-than-satisfactory career with the railways, attendant hobbies and a happy, if rather late, marriage. Oh, and his skin condition cleared up, too.

One never really knows, of course, what traces may have been left by what experience. Statistically, people who have been through serious physical traumas or illnesses, even though they may appear for decades to be entirely recovered, tend to die rather earlier, and often more unexpectedly, than a counterpart in apparently comparable health. It is as if we really do have some inborn quota of strength that is used up sooner in some lives than in others, though it would be difficult to set up any clinical trial to confirm this.

He was eight-and-a-half years younger than me. Although our lives did not intersect a great deal, we saw each other several times a year, usually organised as family occasions that, with the passage of years, came to include grandchildren, N's great-nephews. We exchanged views and concerns regarding our beloved Aunt Monica and Our Mutual Father, and I sought N's advice and opinion on anything I was writing to do with transport. I thought he would always be there for me. In his sixties, he seemed a slim, active, healthy man, a clear linear descendant of a father and grandfather (Bertie) both of whom lived into their nineties. He suffered intermittently from a 'bad back', but who doesn't have some such minor problem as they approach old age? When, one autumn, he began feeling less well than usual and losing strength, he was only reluctantly persuaded by the back-specialist and by his wife that a visit to his GP might be in order soon – no urgency, he felt.

Always a great walker, and regarding walking as a general means of feeling better, one morning he made an accustomed circuit. He bought a few items of food that the house needed, collected and delivered the daily paper to an elderly neighbour, came home – and lay down feeling unusually tired and lacking in appetite for any lunch. He said he would have a sleep, and did. But this sleep turned out to be eternal.

The post-mortem revealed a substantial collapse of the mitral heart valve, which governs the flow of blood from one ventricle to another. I have been told that, in a living man, the onset of this rapidly fatal condition is not easy to diagnose.

Monica's words come back to me:

> *… My heart has been broken*
> *But broken clean, not chimbled. Now it is mended.*
> *A firmly riveted cup …*

We have inherited from so many past centuries, so many poets and tellers of tales, so many casual remarks on calamity, the concept that the human heart can 'break', so that when N's – to all intents and purposes – did, I inevitably wondered if his fractured childhood had finally taken its hidden toll on him.

I do not believe this to be literally the case. I am an inheritor of modern medicine. I understand, approximately, how the human body functions. I know that the true seat of emotion is not in the breast (another huge corpus of images there, to do with feelings), but within the skull. Nevertheless ... I revert again to the odd, observed fact that some sort of assault on personal well-being may have an effect decades later that no one can predict or even analyse.

Since childhood, N had dealt with pain by escaping – into playing the piano, which he did well by ear, into playing with trains, into travelling the world to take photographs, into being an extremely private person. The rare times I attempted to talk to him about his and my own childhoods, he resisted by unobtrusively changing the subject. That was the way he coped.

Now, I feel, he has achieved the ultimate escape. He died lying on his bed in jeans, in a sleep apparently undisturbed by any sudden grimace or cry of distress, with his wife downstairs thinking he would wake up soon, and with plans being made for a seventieth-birthday family lunch for him at the end of the month. Very few of us will achieve an exit from our busy, rewarding, troubled lives as easy and swift as his. After everything, in the end, fortunate N.

Fortunate white ashes lying among the spring flowers of a railway line where trains run no more.

Notes

1. J.W. Dunne's *An Experiment with Time* was first published in 1927, and in numerous subsequent editions and with sequels. His work on time as circular rather than linear, and on precognitive dreams, attracted considerable popular interest and inspired three plays by J.B. Priestley.
2. Jorge Luis Borges, *Labyrinths*, 'The Witness', 1962.
3. *Troilus and Cressida* by Shakespeare, Act III, Scene 2.
4. In 2018 Cuthbert's book figured in the British Library Exhibition, *Anglo-Saxon Kingdoms: Art, Word, War*. It has also generated its own book-about-the-book: *The St Cuthbert Gospel: Studies on the insular manuscript of the Gospel of St John*, eds Claire Breay and Bernard Meeham, 2015.
5. See *The Times*, 25th August 2017.
6. Frédéric Boissonnas (1858–1946) founded his own photographic studio in Geneva. When well on in life he made several major professional expeditions to Greece and the Near East.
7. In the interests of physical preservation, Claydon House archives are not generally available for handling. Microfilmed

copies are variously available in the Bodleian Library in
Oxford, in the British Library, at the Centre for
Buckinghamshire Studies and at several American univer-
sities, including Yale.

8. Nancy Mitford, *The Stanleys of Alderley*, 1939.

9. Professor Andrew Wathey.

10. Danny Braverman. He called his one-man show *What? No Fish!* after a slogan that was often scrawled on wartime walls making a joke out of the chronic food-scarcities.

11. The title of the film is actually a misquotation, deliberate or otherwise, of a line in Laurence Binyon's poem 'For the Fallen', familiar from memorial ceremonies, which runs: 'They shall grow not old …'

12. Personal communication made briefly at a public lecture at the Royal Society of Literature in 2018, by Philippe Sands, QC.

13. Professor Warwick James Rodwell, OBE.

14. Herbert Butterfield, *The Historical Novel*, 1924.

15. By Gauvin Alexander Bailey, Jean Michel Massing and Nuno Vassallo e Silva, Lisbon, 2013. With thanks to Dr Dora Thornton, then curator of the Waddesdon Bequest in the British Museum, who passed me a copy of this article.

16. Dr Holly Trusted [aka Marjorie Trusted], FSA. See 'Survivors of a Shipwreck: Ivories from a Manila Galleon of 1601', *Hispanic Research Journal*, Vol. 14, No. 5, 2013.

17. First published in English by Sinclair-Stevenson, 1995, subsequently by Vintage, and in French as *Célestine, Histoire d'une Femme du Berry*, by Anatolia, Editions du Rocher, 2000.

18. Banziger Hulme Gallery, The Corso, Manly, New South Wales, Australia.

19. Daniel Halévy, *Visites aux Paysans du Centre*, Paris, 1934.

20. *An Autobiography & Other Essays*, 1949.

21. See *Footprints in Paris: A few streets, a few lives*, 2009.

22. Ibid.

23. In *The Book of Laughter and Forgetting*, 1979, which was written in Czech but initially published in a French translation, because its themes were not acceptable to the then-prevailing regime in Czechoslovakia.

24. See Chapter IV.

25. Psalm 137.

26. See the Bible, The Book of Esther.

27. Not his actual name.

28. In the 1990s two separate clinical trials were run, in Wales and Oxfordshire, to establish the effect on sufferers from Post-Traumatic Stress Disorder of getting them to talk about their bad experiences, with control-groups for comparison who received no such attention. The findings were not as expected. The chief psychiatrist involved, Dr Jonathan Bisson, noted that 'the debriefing had not prevented psychological problems at all. In fact, those that received the debriefings fared worse than those that received nothing ... It is possible that the debriefing actually contributes to the patient getting PTSD.'

29. Richard Crossman (1907–1974).

30. *Daily Telegraph*, 21st June 1866, headed 'Neighbourly Relations.'

31. *The Fields Beneath: The history of one London village*. First published 1977 and in several different editions since.

32. *Assassin's Creed*, described by its proprietors, Ubisoft, as 'an action-adventure stealth-video game ... It depicts the

centuries-old struggle between the Assassins and the Templars ... ' It has spawned books, comics and a film.

33. The father was the minister in Lochell, and the son was Charles Forbes, who (unlike an elder brother) survived. The father did not, indeed, live long enough to see his boy again, but Charles prospered considerably, became a notable Bombay citizen and finally returned to England, became an MP and eventually a baronet.

34. See Dickens's *Our Mutual Friend* (1865, but set back in time), in which the Golden Dustman has inherited a vast, valuable rubbish tip by King's Cross.

35. By a Canadian, Major John McCrae. He is thought to have written the poem in 1915, after he had had to conduct a burial service for a close friend killed in action.

36. Eamon Duffy, *The Stripping of the Altars: Traditional religion in England c.1400–1580*, 1992.

37. Up to date information from Professor Turi King of the University of Leicester, in a lecture given at the Royal Institute in November 2018.

38. Anthony Adolph, *Brutus of Troy: And the quest for the ancestry of the British*, 2016.

39. T.D. Kendrick (Sir Thomas Downing Kendrick, KCB, 1895–1979).

40. See *This Orient Isle: Elizabethan England and the Islamic World* by Jerry Brotton, 2016.

41. *Wonderful Adventures of Mrs Seacole in Many Lands* 1857.

42. See *Le Soldat Inconnu Vivant* by Jean-Yves le Naour, Paris, 2002.

43. The first line of a poem by Rupert Brooke, who was to die in 1915.

44. *My Boy Jack?* by Tonie and Valmai Holt, 1998, and subsequent revised editions.

45. Actually Felsted. It was another member of the extended family who went to Haileybury.

46. Walter Savage Landor, *Imaginary Conversations: Aesop and Rhodope*, 1844.

47. Edward Richardson (1812–1869).

48. See *The Life of Walter de la Mare* by Theresa Whistler, 2004.

49. This letter is attributed, in *The History of the Families of Jacob*, to the year 1814, but from its internal evidence about her state of health, this cannot be correct.

50. Dean Street Press, Salisbury.

51. Émile Durkheim, *Suicide*, first published in French, 1897.

52. Dean Street Press, as above.

Further Reading

All books published in London unless otherwise stated.

Adeane, Jane E. and Grenfell, Maud (eds), *Before and After Waterloo: Letters from Edward Stanley, sometime Bishop of Norwich (1802, 1814, 1816)*, 1907.

Adeane, J.H. (ed.), *The Girlhood of Maria Josepha Holroyd*, 1896.

Bevan, Robert, *The Destruction of Memory: Architecture and war*, 2006.

Borges, Jorge Luis, *Labyrinths*, 1962.

Davies, Norman (ed.), *The Paston Letters*, Oxford 1958.

Duffy, Eamon, *The Stripping of the Altars: Traditional religion in England c.1400–1580*, 1992.

Higgins, Charlotte, *Under Another Sky: Journeys into Roman Britain*, 2013.

Hillary, Richard, *The Last Enemy*, 1942.

Kundera, Milan, *The Book of Laughter and Forgetting*, 1979.

Le Goff, Jacques, *La Naissance du Purgatoire*, 1981 (in English, 1984).

Licence, Tom, *What the Victorians Threw Away*, Oxford 2015.

Nabokov, Vladimir, *Speak, Memory*, 1967.

O'Brien, Tim, *The Things They Carried*, 1990.

Orlando, Francesco, *Obsolete Objects in the Literary Imagination: Ruins, relics, rarities, rubbish, uninhabited places, and hidden treasures*, 1993 (in English, 2006).

Packard, Vance, *The Waste Makers*, 1960.

Plumb, J.H., *The Death of the Past*, 1969.

Rieff, David, *In Praise of Forgetting*, 2016.

Rutherford, Adam, *A Brief History of Everyone Who Ever Lived*, 2016.

Sweet, Rosemary, *Antiquaries: The discovery of the past in eighteenth-century Britain*, 2004.

Thompson, Michael, *Rubbish Theory: The creation and destruction of value*, 1979.

Trevelyan, G.M., *English Social History: A Survey of Six Centuries, Chancer to Victoria*, 1944.

Tuchman, Barbara, *August 1914*, 1962.

Verney, Lady Margaret (ed.), *The Verney Letters of the Eighteenth Century*, 1930.

Verney, Lady Parthenope (ed.), *Memoirs of the Verney Family during the Seventeenth Century*, 1904.

Verney, Sir Harry (ed.), *The Verneys of Claydon: A seventeenth century English family*, 1968.

Acknowledgements

In addition to my supportive publishers, and my agent Gordon Wise, I am indebted to a number of people who have contributed to the writing of this book, sometimes knowingly by their interest and advice, but often unawares – by mentioning something I hadn't thought of, introducing me to an idea or a piece of knowledge, allowing me to experience their habitat, lending me a document, sharing a childhood memory with me, or by preserving an object or handing on a factual account that would otherwise have been lost or gone. In alphabetical order they are: Anthony Adolph, Tudor Allen, Peter Barber, Jack Black, Roger Cazalet, Francesca Cioci, Leonard Fenton, Marie-Joseph Gardez de Soos and her family, Nicholas Hale, Sean Hardie, Sheila Jones, Anthony Kaye, Paul Lay, Donald Maddox, Stacy Marking, Pierre Menet, Fiorella Morandi, Jan Patterson, Marie-France de Perronet and her family, Silvie Pirot, Munro Price, Jeremy Seabrook, Mike Shaw, Scott Thompson, Colin Thubron, David Wenk.

And I am equally indebted to a growing number of people I used to know, and whose own knowledge, memories and influence have fed into this and other of my books, but who I do not list here by name as they are no longer alive to read my thanks to them and have become themselves part of the huge panoply of the past, outside the confines of time.

Index